Southern Cunning

Folkloric Witchcraft in the
American South

Southern Cunning

Folkloric Witchcraft in the American South

Aaron Oberon

MOON
BOOKS

Winchester, UK
Washington, USA

First published by Moon Books, 2019
Moon Books is an imprint of John Hunt Publishing Ltd., No. 3 East Street, Alresford
Hampshire SO24 9EE, UK
office1@jhpbooks.net
www.johnhuntpublishing.com
www.moon-books.net

For distributor details and how to order please visit the 'Ordering' section on our website.

ISBN: 978 1 78904 196 5
978 1 78904 197 2 (ebook)
Library of Congress Control Number: 2018952687

A CIP catalogue record for this book is available from the British Library.

Design: Stuart Davies

UK: Printed and bound by TJ Books Limited, Padstow, Cornwall
US: Printed and bound by Thomson-Shore, 7300 West Joy Road, Dexter, MI 48130

MIX
Paper | Supporting
responsible forestry
FSC® C013056

We operate a distinctive and ethical publishing philosophy in
all areas of our business, from our global network of authors to
production and worldwide distribution.

Contents

Acknowledgments

This project has been in the back of my mind for years. It wasn't until I started listening to a certain podcast that this really took off. *New World Witchery* has my eternal gratitude for showing me that there are smart, funny, and passionate witches out there searching for the same thing I am. Cory and Laine are wonderful folks who have been wonderful resources and are infinitely humble in regards to the impact they are making in the world of witchcraft. Through their podcast I also found *Down at the Crossroads*, another podcast of witches on a traditional walk. Their work in bioregionalism was another massive push for me. Their approach to land spirits as central magical figures (namely the importance they put on the Jersey Devil) solidified my long held belief that the stories we grew up with contain power.

The work of Sarah Anne Lawless has inspired an entire generation of traditional witches and I count myself among them. She's another one who has always put information out there in a genuine and very kind way. Her work on spirit vessels and flying ointments made a massive shift in my practice. I use her ancestor vessel design for my own ancestors. My thanks to Sarah Anne Lawless for all the work she has put out there.

My biggest thanks goes to my partner, The Historian. Not just for his love and support, but his wealth of knowledge about our state and bioregion. He's bought me books on local folklore, told me stories he grew up with, and helped me stay true to my purpose. I love you.

Then of course there are my two dear friends who have been my cheerleaders from the get go. Alex McCartney and Sigrún Haljoruna. Sigrún and I began our more traditional paths together, and your support in this lonely practice has helped me survive. Alex is truly a brother in the craft, and our talks have both warmed my heart and killed my data plan. Thank you for reading the draft copies and helping me make the most true to form version of this book.

To Lee Harrington for taking a chance on me and giving me invaluable advice. Lee accepted my submission to *Queer Magic* in December of 2016, a year after I started this project. That essay (*A Drag Queen Possessed*) lit a fire under my ass to make this book a reality. Lee helped me get used to editing and helped ground me in the reality of what to expect through this process.

The Witch Father, maker of witches. Skin stripper, bone eater, wild man, stag head. You pulled the stars from the sky to show me this way. You threw me around and pulled the poison from my body. This is your book. It always has been.

Chapter One

Searching for Witchcraft in the Stories of the South

There are devils living in the dirt. There are dead men forced into the shape of beetles and women who command them. There are men who shoot the sun with silver bullets and greet the devil as an old friend. There are mothers who go through super markets buying herbs for healing and herbs for cursing. There are brothers who go out at midnight and bury bottles at the crossroads. There are witches in them hills, by the swamps, and in your apartment complex.

For many of us, the witches of folklore are not just characters in books; they are our inspirations, our aspirations, and our ancestors. Contemporary witchcraft is a hodgepodge of practices from around the world. It is a mix of religions, social movements, and revitalizations. Some of us witches have been taught that witchcraft is about four corners and gods, but that may not ring true for everyone. Some contemporary witches grew up on stories about hags cursing those who did them wrong and thought, "I want to be like her."

Folkloric witchcraft is a stream of traditional witchcraft that is firmly rooted in folklore and bioregionalism. I call it a stream because it doesn't fit quite so neatly into what is considered traditional witchcraft and because it avoids a mess of confusion with capital letters. Folkloric witchcraft isn't necessarily as concerned with historical accuracy, as is proper traditional witchcraft, instead, it focuses on personal authenticity and accountability. It's about remembering those witches in folk tales and creating our own witchcraft and folk tales today. It is witchcraft rooted in folklore and blooming where we land.

Us American witches grew up hearing urban legends,

campfire stories, and tales of haunted houses in the places we lived and never batted an eye. We were taught that these were "just stories" by other contemporary witches, and that mythology or pre-Christian religion is the one true wellspring of all witchcraft. Traditional witchcraft came at about the same time as contemporary witchcraft, but differed in that it argued that witchcraft was a largely secular practice that often intertwined pre-Christian and Christian world views.

I was first exposed to witchcraft through scary stories, the Bible, and television. I grew up in the South and learned ways to read the Psalms to make things go my way and I even learned how to put the right objects into bags to make things I didn't like go away. I took what I saw on TV or heard in a story and made it work for me. Then, I met contemporary witches and they told me I was doing it wrong. I was told that I needed to work with the classical elements and throw out my Bible. I was told that to be a witch, I needed to be Wiccan. I was told to pick out names from a book of mythology and invoke these chosen names as my patrons. I saw the way that these other witches grew through these same methods and I wanted to be like them. However, I didn't grow magically for years because I continually tried to force myself into someone else's box.

Eventually, I came across folk magic and saw some awfully familiar things – Cunning Folk who used psalms to cure and witches who lived in swamps and made magic bags. I met folks who called themselves traditional witches, and things started to fall in line. A little. I brought back all the things I started with and challenged the norms of the witchcraft around me. I started searching for a witchcraft that felt organic. I realized real quickly that I wasn't alone.

At its heart, this book is an exploration. It isn't a how-to or a claim of unbroken lines of witchcraft. This is a case study; an example of how I looked back on where I grew up and the stories of that place, the stories that my parents and grandparents heard, and how the land I lived on guided me from a young age without my knowing. I want to look at folklore as a source of power, the land as a teacher, and my ancestors as starting points. Most importantly, this book is for anyone who is looking at the witchcraft that has been presented to them and says, "That doesn't look anything like me."

In writing this book, I went through one of the most prominent examples of witch lore in the United States, *The Silver Bullet*. From this work, I began to piece together a cohesive practice based on what was presented and from my personal experience. With that in mind, this book acts as an examination of *The Silver Bullet*, and the practice I have formed around it over the course of several years. Case studies should provide the reader with insights as to how these tools can be applied, but it is not an absolute guide to folkloric witchcraft. Most of the time, what was in the stories could not be translated literally or done by me. Generally, that was because a story involved boiling a cat alive, shooting a gun into the air, or anything else that common sense today says not to do.

The goal isn't to perfectly mimic what the folklore presents, otherwise what would be the point in grounding it to where I live? Rather, the goal is to look at folklore and urban legends as things intimately tied to where we live. This book is mostly for witches in the United States, and more specifically in the South. The general idea, however, can be applied to any region around the world with the idea being that the stories we tell have power, and that where we tell those stories helps bring them to life.

Additionally, I want this to be practical and something that readers can look at and understand. Most books on traditional witchcraft are very poetic, academic, and formal. Academics are incredibly important in traditional witchcraft, but can be alienating and create a lot of "armchair witchcraft". Similarly, poetic books on witchcraft often focus on deep mysteries and can come off to the reader as pretentious, even if that's not the intention. Formality can be great, but the crossover between all three of these things has given traditional witchcraft a certain reputation. Basically, there is an air of absolute and required seriousness that pervades the traditional witchcraft world, along with a lot of people who fall back on the statement, "You wouldn't understand."

I've been there and I even tried to make this book fit that mold. However, when I was writing like that, I wasn't writing anything of substance. I'm not a brooding or very serious person. I was raised in a poor, rural town in Central Florida, and I went to a private college where I was labeled a backwoods hick. It was difficult for some folks to hear academic jargon coming out of my mouth without immediately discrediting what I was saying because of my accent. The writing of this book reflects my education and my upbringing – tight sections of citation and academic background, with a whole lot of "Y'all ain't gon' believe this!" thrown in.

To try and make this something flowery and cosmically profound just doesn't work with who I am as a person, where I come from, or the stories that came with it. If we idolize the cranky ole' hag of folklore but use language she would side eye at, who are we trying to impress?

What this is

For the most part, this book is a head first dive into *The Silver Bullet*. You'll find versions of the rituals in that book that make sense for a witch today. You'll also find bits of folk magic, modern ideas about spirits, devil talk, leaving your skin behind, familiar spirits, and hopefully, a sense of humor about what we witches do. You'll find plenty of serious and potentially life changing events, but don't think for a second that some kooky shit don't happen when dead folks are involved.

You may also find some aspects of this book you're already familiar with that are pulled from other streams of magic.

For example, influences from grimoires, conjure, folk magic, cunning craft, and others wormed their way into the pages and found a home. All these bits of magic also influenced the folklore collected in *The Silver Bullet*, but that doesn't mean you'll learn any of those traditions in and of themselves. Those things are learned from people and spirits, not a book.

This book can provide you with tools to look at your folklore and say, "There's something more to that" and bring it into your craft. You'll learn how to approach land spirits and how to listen to them. You'll learn ways to hex a lousy neighbor and how to use the crossroads to meet with a certain Ole' Man. You'll learn how initiation from spirits can impact you, and hopefully, you already have the common sense to decide if it's really what you want.

The rituals pulled from *The Silver Bullet* are written as an "ideal" way to do them meaning that they're written as if you have access to everything described. I do this for a few reasons, mainly because I can't possibly write every single potential scenario that may occur. By writing the rituals from an idealized perspective you, the reader, can look at something and say, *"Well that ain't gonna work so I'll do it this way."* I'll list some changes I've made along the way along with some personal experiences, but there's a reason I only focus on *The Silver Bullet* and not all the other folklore that's out there. I actually wanted to finish the book. If I didn't narrow it down, it would never have made it into your lovely hands.

What this ain't

This book isn't always comfortable. Folklore is nasty, and witches are nastier; they have always been curse slingers, shapeshifters, and rule benders. Now, I'm not as nasty as some of those lovely ladies, but I don't shy away from who they are. You won't find much sugar coating in this book. We might not perfectly mirror the old witches, but we sure are inspired by them. To that end, you won't find the familiar distinguishing features of most contemporary witchcraft. There are no gods or goddesses, no elements or watch towers, and no seasonal celebrations. There's no paganism in this book. This is not to say pagans can't practice this way, but rather that *anyone* from *any* background can practice this way. How you handle your religion and witchcraft ain't my business.

I also won't be denigrating Christianity. The Bible is a massive influence on witchcraft, whether we like it or not. In fact, I use the Bible in almost all of my witchcraft and it will be featured throughout the book. It's not religious in this context, but it's also not stripped of its religious perspective. It's very likely some folk reading this will have an uncomfortable relationship with Christianity and may even feel uncomfortable reading about it in this book. I hope that more witches get used to being uncomfortable and address why these between states are uncomfortable.

Most importantly, let me spell out that this book has nothing to do with so-called "Confederate Pride" or any other excuse for white supremacy. By including the word "Southern" in the title of this book there are going to be some misguided folks who want to use this material the wrong way. The South is a place filled with people from all over the world and ultimately, the South wouldn't exist without people of color. Southerners should be bound together by hospitality, comfort food, and an understanding of the land. Furthermore, European decedents (white folks) should be using their places of privilege to shut down any notion that the South is a white experience. So, if you picked this up intending to have some kind of Southern, White Witch Wonderbread fantasy, put it down.

What makes the Witch?

Witches today can't agree on what a witch is. However, folklore and anthropology are relatively clear on what witchcraft is: magic done to harm someone or something. To them, witchcraft is magic that does a bad thing. So, do we as contemporary witches have to accept that as the way we ourselves think of witches today? No, as long as we realize that almost the entire world thinks otherwise.

"Witch" is a reclaimed slur. It has always been a negative thing, and in most places, it is still a negative thing. Depending on where I travel, I go from being a witch to being an ancestral practitioner real fast. When we use the word "witch", we have to know what its historical meaning is, especially if we plan on inverting it in some way.

In a book on witchcraft, there has to be some kind of definition as to what a witch is. Whether you agree with the definition I give ain't important, but if there's no definition to set things straight, then the perspective may be confusing. I'll define "witch", and then define what a folkloric witch is within the confines of this book.

To help define what a witch is, I did a short catalogue of various elements that take place in initiation rituals of *The Silver Bullet*. These tales give us a solid read on the views of the general Southern population concerning witches. I went through these stories to find the most common themes on what makes a witch and, most importantly, to answer the question "What did witches in folklore do?"

They cursed. They cursed a lot. In seventeen out of twenty-four stories, witches are cursing someone. The cursed cows, butter, kids, and guns. They were able to do all this cursin' because they had been initiated into witchcraft by the Devil through various rituals. As shown in folklore, a witch is someone who gains power from the Devil and utilizes that power most often to curse, and always to further their own goals.

That is what we see in folklore; however, we do not live within our folklore. So, what matters to us is how we define what a witch is within the context of this book. For the goal of this book, a witch is someone who attains power from otherworldly entities to be used in whichever way they see fit. It's important to go through the stories and the information because that allows us to know the rules. When you know the rules, you can break them accordingly.

Definitions and Terms of Importance

For clarity, there are some other terms that I use specifically throughout the book that could use some defining.

- *Contemporary witchcraft* refers to the entire body of witchcraft being practiced in the contemporary era (1945-present) which includes folkloric witchcraft, Traditional Witchcraft, and Wicca. Ultimately, it's a broad term that refers to a specific time frame, though not a specific tradition or approach.
- *Early Modern Witchcraft* is historically attested witchcraft beliefs and practices found throughout trial records, historical documents, and archeological research. Early Modern Witchcraft is frequently looked to for inspiration in contemporary witchcraft practices as there is a wealth of information surrounding witchcraft during this time.
- *Traditional Witchcraft* is lineaged non-Wiccan witchcraft. Traditional Witchcraft often includes a coven structure and very specific ritual techniques that vary little between person to person. Conversely, *traditional witchcraft* refers to non-lineaged, non-Wiccan witchcraft that draws on history, folklore, and bioregionalism as influences.
- *Folkloric witchcraft* is a term I use to replace lower-case traditional witchcraft which focuses primarily on local folklore, ancestral traditions, and bioregionalism to inform a person's witchcraft. Both folkloric and traditional witchcraft are individualized practices, often lacking any kind of coven or group structure and has high amounts of variety between practitioners who claim the terms.

Now, folks may not agree on the specifics of all these terms and that's quite alright. Witches are finicky creatures, and we have very strong opinions on what things mean. Take the terms as I use them for this book and then draw your own conclusions.

Folk Witch

A folk witch speaks with the dead. They know the stories and build upon them. They keep a familiar spirit who is the witches' seat of power. Folklore is how we enact that power. A folk witch isn't initiated by flesh; rather, a folk witch learns from the story of Jonas Dotson. A folk witch is initiated by spirit. This initiator was originally called *the* Devil, but it's probably more honest to call this initiator *a* devil; one of many.

Beyond any of that, a folk witch is someone who holds themselves accountable, learning to tread the line of what can and cannot be changed, in both practice and life. Honesty is what propels folk witches forward – honesty with other witches, with the spirits, and with yourself. That's not to say that a folk witch is an open book as there are still secrets to be had. But, a folk witch isn't someone to say what they do is authentic over what another does, or tell other witches what they're doing is wrong. A folk witch knows, *"what you eat don't make me shit."*

Chapter Two

Omens, Dreams, and Divination – Languages of the Spirits

Dealing with other people is all about communication. Communication is how we build upon every single relationship we maintain. With spirits, it's exactly the same. During initiation rituals, the initiating spirit communicates through omens. Omens are essentially signs from spirits that confirm, advise, or warn the person observing them. What gives an omen power is that we, as humans, have no influence over them. We may interpret them incorrectly or even see them where they don't exist, but we can't force them to happen.

In the story of the bloody sunrise, the prospective witch needs to complete an initiation ritual then wait for the sun to rise dripping blood. When it comes to spirit initiation, the only way we can know if we have truly been accepted is through omen taking. Omen taking allows us to stay honest with ourselves because to wait for a sign and not receive it means we have to rethink what we are doing.

Omens are not cut and dry. They rely on a lot of factors, the foremost being that you can't be expecting them. If you're doing a ritual and the omen is a blood moon or a bloody sunrise and you wait to do the ritual till you know a blood moon is taking place, then you have not taken an omen. We have to let omens come to us organically. This is a strong reminder of our witchcraft.

An exhaustive list of omens won't do an individual any help. For example, I could say that seeing a blue jay means you've been visited by an ancestor, but if you live in the middle of several blue jay nesting areas, does that really give you any unique insight? Each witch should create their own understanding of omens by reading folklore, asking spirits, and most importantly, knowing their region.

Understanding Omens Regionally

Our practice is twofold, one being folklore and the other being bioregionalism. Omen taking combines these two perfectly and makes a wonderful starting place for understanding a regional witchcraft. Take time to learn as much as possible about the place you live. One way to do this is by reading books on the bioregion (the region as defined by nature, not man-made or cultural spaces). These books will give you an understanding of what's normal in your area, what animals are common, which are rare, and at what times they are more or less likely to be around humans.

I have lived in some very different bioregions. I grew up in southern Maryland where there are plenty of woods and forests that are reasonably safe to explore. There were very few animals that would harm you, and I have literally run with deer on multiple occasions but when I moved to central Florida as a teenager, that changed dramatically. Everything in Florida wants to eat you! Swimming in a lake is an invitation to feed an alligator for the day and there are snakes literally everywhere. The swamp also wants to drown you and use you to grow more cypress. Basically, the way I practiced living on the edge of a swamp versus the edge of a wooded suburb was very different. I spent about ten years going back and forth between those two places and my practice simply did not look the same.

In Florida, seeing dangerous wildlife was common as I lived in a town famous for its lakes and the alligators they contained. In Maryland, deer could pop out of your neighbor's yard and steal your dog's food. So, when it came to omen taking, things had to change. To begin, it can help to write a list down of both common and uncommon natural occurrences. I've mostly focused on animal life, but weather and seasonal changes should be kept in mind as well. There are Southern expressions about rain and sunshine meaning the Devil is beating his wife. That complicated saying has spurred a lot of thinking for me. Explore all those things to create a list of omens that are meaningful to you and your spirits.

On Asking for Omens

I place different emphasis on omens depending on how I have asked for them. There are many times when I receive omens with no prompting, but most of the time, I take notice after asking for one. The most basic form is something we've all done: "Please give me a sign that I'm on the right path." This is the most basic way to ask for an omen, and most of the time, the response is something just as casual and subtle such as finding a feather shortly after, or having a stranger say something kind. However, when witchcraft is mixed in, things become more direct.

Asking for omens regarding magical work can be similar to asking for life questions. This is, after all, a form of divination in its own right. The most common occurrence of this is during your initiation rituals. The entire rite itself is one huge request for an omen. That omen comes in a huge way, something celestial. We cannot force a star to fall or the moon to bleed – only spirits of great power could manage that. This is an example of requests equaling the intensity of an omen.

Divination

Omen taking is just one way in which spirits talks to us. Omens primarily serve as a form of communication during initiation and other life changing events. Other times when we want answers from spirits, we should develop a practice of divination. *The Silver Bullet* gives one example of playing cards having magical meaning, and is a very old form of divination[1]. The versatility that comes from cartomancy is something that makes the system so appealing to folk witches. The damn things are everywhere. There are common meanings, but there's no artist interpretation to stop you from really creating your own way of working with the cards. You can play poker with the cards you read to give them practical experience with the spirits of others. Playing poker could be a kind of ritual itself for empowering the spirits of the cards.

Tarot is almost synonymous with divination and witches. It's the first system I learned and has hundreds of books covering it. What's nice about tarot is that if one deck doesn't work for you, you can find one that will. There are hundreds of different decks with slightly different approaches. In fact, you may even find that certain decks work better for certain kinds of readings and start specializing with them.

Throwing bones to determine fate is one of the most iconic magical images. This can be as simple and as complicated as the set builder makes it. Just like with omen taking the pieces have to have meanings agreed upon by the witch and the spirits at play. Specially marked cloths may become a part of the process, or just the proximity each bone has with each other. When kept in mind for the *Rite of the Rescued Animal* there are many opportunities to build upon spirit relations with bone reading.

Dreams

About twice a year, I get a phone call from my mother warning me about something that hasn't happened yet. She never gives me details, she just calls and says, "You better talk to your grandmother. I had a dream and you need to call." These calls always end up being good advice and what little details she does give are always true. My mother isn't a psychic; she doesn't even believe in magic, and on more than one occasion she has worried for my eternal soul. However, she does believe in the power of dreams and visions with the conviction of any psychic or witch I've ever met.

Dreams have meaning to Southerners. Often, Southern folk don't make any question about why they matter, they just do.

You dream about a family member getting sick, you call them and check up on them. You dream about your car breaking down, you take it to the shop. Dolly Parton's momma in the movie, *The Coat of Many Colors* even had prophetic dreams, and it made for the best scene in the whole damn movie. That movie also gives an insight as to why Southerners may not think twice about the power of dreams.

In the Bible, there was a man named Joseph, who wore a coat of many colors, that had dreams sent to him by God warning him of many things. The logic is that if it's in the Bible, done by a righteous man, and sent by God, then it must be okay. Growing up, I often heard Southern women talking about their dreams and how they came true. These dreams are almost always warning of something dire, most often sickness.

These kinds of dreams have been major milestones for me throughout my life. I've had dreams warn me of certain people who would steal from me, jobs that would be bad for me, and even roads that I should avoid while driving. I've also had dreams where spirits speak to me, advise me, and teach me. I always record the happenings in a dream and make sure to go back to them from times to time.

I think that dreams tend to be the place where we are the least resistant to spirits. We are creatures full of doubt, and this closes us off from experiences because we are often so afraid of our craft not being real. In dreams, spirits can come and speak to us without the burden of our doubt keeping us from listening. So, while a witch is developing their path, dreams become that much more important.

Dreams are not something that we can control. We can ask for prophetic dreams, do rituals before sleep, and even set preparations to fly during our sleep but as more seasoned witches know, dreams are unpredictable things. There is no set way to ensure a dream is prophetic, but there are things that can be done to petition our spirits to open our dreams more.

You can sleep with a skeleton key under your pillow to increase your chances of flight during sleep. You can wrap a horseshoe in white cloth and place it under your pillow to speak with the Devil's Wife during your sleep. You can leave a glass of water out and ask your ancestors for visions during your sleep. You can combine any of these with direct requests to your familiar spirits to what you want to take place during your sleep.

None of these are guaranteed, however, and I find that the more rigorously you try to force prophetic dreams, the less likely you are to receive them. I'm not sure the reason why, that's just my experience. However, the times when I've whispered to my spirits, "Take me on a journey tonight" before sleep with an amulet under my pillow, I've had great success. More often than not, you'll receive them when they're needed though.

Chapter Three

Protections

Protective magic is a pretty big deal in contemporary witchcraft, in fact the characterizing practice of an entire witchcraft-derived religion is the inclusion of the protective circle. This can be the breaking point for a lot of witches I've come to discover. The use of the circle is something a lot of witches are very passionate about, to the point where some claim you can't call something witchcraft without using a circle. The idea that a single element of practice (in this case circles) is the marking point of what makes something "not witchcraft" is hogwash and most folks won't pay that any mind. But protection is a serious question for folks who are used to Wicca-derived witchcraft and may be interested in folkloric witchcraft.

Folkloric witches don't use circles the way most Wiccan folks do. Circles do pop up in folklore but not too often. Circles appear almost always when something is being conjured. Witches looking to meet the Devil drew a circle in the dirt and danced around it till he appeared.[1] So when folkloric witches do use circles it's not to close out forces but rather to create a liminal space to interact with specific spirits. Even then, I prefer the crossroads approach rather than a circle. Crossroads are inherently liminal, whereas circles are closed off and would need to become liminal to accomplish the same goal for a folk witch.

For me protection is not a ritualized practice incorporated into every work, but rather a day to day maintenance. I think of spiritual protection the same way I think of physical protection. If I felt unsafe for my home I would have a home security system, locks on the windows and doors, and a baseball bat in case someone actually does break in. I also have outdoor lights that scare away would be intruders and I don't live alone so I have the security of someone else there. Spiritually, I have a witch bottle hidden on my property to distract would be attackers that alerts me when someone gets caught (home security system). I have various talismans hidden in places that block outside forces (locks on the door). I have a Devil's Club in case someone gets frisky (baseball bat). Most importantly I have familiar spirits who are always with me to scare off (outside lights) and support me (never alone) if someone ever tried to interfere with my home.

What I like about this approach is that it's one and done. I put up a witch bottle and unless someone tampers with it, I don't have to worry about that bottle anymore. I check it periodically just like everything else and replace it when need be. I don't have to worry about building a ritual circle for every work because I am already protected. To continue the home security analogy, a circle is a panic room. No entry and no exit. I don't always need that, but I know how to get one if need be. I'll address these and a few other forms of protection that come from both folklore and personal experience.

Cleansing

This may be surprising, but I truly feel that a lite cleansing is the first step to protecting a home. This comes in part from new age philosophies and partially from ancestral folk practices of Ireland. Cleansing can be done by smoke (rosemary is a good choice for age old purification associations) or by water. A trick that I was taught by my born-again Christian hippie sister is to take a white candle and a bowl of water and walk from room to room asking negative energy to either be transformed by the light or absorbed into the water. Finish off with psalms to ensure the place is blessed and ready to go. She taught me this at a young age and it really stuck with me. Despite obvious new age influences, I consider it as much an influence as bible magic was on me.

Another more modern approach to cleansing is the use of

tinctures in a spray bottle. Take cleansing herbs (rosemary, birch, and juniper is my personal blend) and let it soak in high-proof vodka or grain alcohol for several days. Strain and put into a spray bottle to disperse for whatever cleansing needs. I feel like folks would again scoff at the modernity of this, and they can suck an egg because those little bottles work like a charm.

The river cleansing found in the Killing the Moon ritual can be another simple influence on how to clean a home. Take river water and sprinkle a bit around the home to clean it up. If you plan on storing the water for later cleaning, add a dash of alcohol to give it a little more shelf life. Add it to your mop water, or hell even your windex to keep things spiritually clean. What's nice about this is that through the Killing the Moon ritual you have a connection to that source of water and rather than repelling your spirits it can feed them.

Brass, Iron, and Copper

In the story *The Brass Screw*[2] we get a little nugget of information that is pretty useful but never explained. Simply put "For some reason, witches can't spell brass." Brass isn't alone, iron has been a long time source of magical protection and I've always been told that copper is another go to for protective metals. Brass is the only directly stated metal in *Silver Bullet* and in particular it was a brass screw in a gun that prevents a witch from placing a curse on the gun. So brass as a part of something else can, for good or bad, prevent something from being spelled.

Horseshoes

Horseshoes are a favorite decoration throughout the South, hanging horns up above door frames. Different folks will say different thing, but mostly horseshoes are either for safety or luck. So by hanging the horseshoe it pulls in luck and keeps the home safe from unwanted guests.

Witch Bottles

An oldie but a goodie. Piss in a mason jar, throw in broken glass, mirrors, barbed wire, sulfur, and bullets. Bury it somewhere on your property. If a spirit or spell comes looking for you they will mistake the urine for you and get caught in the bottle. Normally one bottle should be good per home, but if you have a knack for pissing off other practitioners you may need to replace it often.

Sator Squares

Sator Squares have been used in magic from Pompeii to Appalachia[3.] Such a long history of use has given this charm an air of mystery and versatility. Normally the charm is written out on clay or paper tablets that are hung up for protection. They work (in my experience) by just keeping unwanted presences out. They don't trap like the bottle, they just don't let things in. I wouldn't keep it by the front door, since it's designed to let things in, but rather put the square in small or hidden entry ways that would only be used by something nasty.

```
S A T O R
A R E P O
T E N E T
O P E R A
R O T A S
```

Spirit Traps

These can take a number of forms but because I'm a sucker for sewn talismans I make mine out of cloth. Every practitioner will put their own spin on this, but there are hints in folklore that can help shape these traps. The main idea is that spirits are compelled to count things. As vague as that sounds it is a very common idea. So I make the designs on these a bit more complex and do a lot of stitching to compel spirits to count the stitches. Then I fill it with Spanish moss, because of how interlocked it is and its nature of being pseudo-parasitic. I weave these traps to draw in a spirit and lock it into the moss. Most counting myths state that spirits are either destroyed or sent away by sunlight. I personally have not experienced this and any spirit caught needs to either be destroyed by the witch (who has time for that?) or banished.

Rocks are another favorite for spirit traps. I brightly paint river rocks (again, drawing a spirits attention) and place a mark on the bottom to trap the spirit. The same idea could be done with mirrors, pots, bottles, you name it.

There is also the chance that you could take control of the spirit, or make a deal with it to join you. I first saw this concept written by the fabulous Sarah Lawless[4] and although enticing I have never felt the desire to do so.

Haint Trees

These beauties are some of the most captivating pieces of art you'll find anywhere. I didn't see them much growing up, mostly just when we'd visit kin up in the Carolinas, but I always loved the blue bottles hanging from empty tree limbs. A haint tree is a tree that has blue bottles (other glass as well) hanging onto or from the limbs. The purpose of the haint tree, as told to me by my auntie, was to catch devils that would try to sneak into your house and leave the devils to get burned up at sunrise.

As a witch, the act of empowering a tree on my land with glass and my own magic is incredibly appealing. This could be a way of directly working with your land and protecting the space in which you live.

Haint Blue, Red Doors, and Harris Green

The reason why haint trees use blue bottles is because of specific folkloric power of the color haint blue. Haint blue is said to drive away evil spirit and wasps. Haint blue is a well-known feature on many Southern porches as well, normally the ceiling of a porch is painted to cover the entry way. In Florida haint blue is not as common, however Harris green takes its place. Easily confused with sea foam green, harris is known for its protection from wasps and other stinging insects. Painting a front door red is another old paint trick to prevent folk with ill intent from coming into your home.

Wards

Not a necessarily a folkloric idea, but one that is very common in most fantasy genre books that has been readily adopted by contemporary witches. The idea here is that it's something that keeps things out. Sator Squares act as a ward in a way. I include this here mostly so that newer witches can cross reference common phrases.

Getting Rid of Nasty Things

Most witches aren't huge fans of the word "demon" to describe spirits that mean harm. Some witches may work exclusively with demons that are helpful towards them. I know a Wiccan who simply called unwanted spirits "Nasties" and I've found that phrase to be perfectly descriptive. Protective forces normally deal with the majority of Nasty Things that may cause trouble, but sometimes things get through the cracks. So you'll need to have ways to get rid of 'em. All four of these things should be on hand but do not necessarily have to be directly apart of your daily craft.

The Witch's Broom

Using the broom can be a gentler form of expulsion. It essentially scoots the spirit out without causing harm. Lost or confused spirits can be easily removed with this by simply going about you daily cleaning with your broom created from the land. If a Nasty is really dedicated though move on to the Devil's club.

The Devil's Club

There is a taboo in folklore that witches who lose their witchballs or give away a covens secrets will get lashed by the Devil with a bundle of thorns.[5] In several other tales, using a bundle of thorns on something that's been witched can not only remove the curse but hurt the witch who's done the witchin'. This aggressive and very specific action got me thinking that a bundle of thorns is a helluva way to deal with nasty spirits. Other magical traditions talk about the use of knives, staves, and wands to get rid of Nasty Things.

Those all work wonderfully, but the Devil's club is unique in that its absolute only job is to tear things up. It is not multipurpose, it exists to take out things that don't belong. It's not gentle, it's nasty and if a little bit of a witchball is added to the bundle I've found that nothing is going to stick around to fight with you.

You make the club by finding a thorny plant. Anything with thorns will do the job but folklore makes specific mention of rose thorns. I usually opt for whatever is prominent in your locality so other options may be bougainvillea, Devil's crown, or hawthorn. Carefully collect sturdy, thin, foot long sticks from the plant of choice. The number of sticks you collect will depend on the specific plant but you'll want the bundle to be a comfortable in your hand. Take some clippers and clean off about five inches of thorns near the base of each stick so you can hold the bundle

22

safely. Carefully position the branches so that you can get a good grip on the cleaned off portion and begin wrapping twine around the soon-to-be handle. Wrap the twine as evenly as possible around the base of the sticks. Tie off the twine with a solid knot and you're good to go. I find that when not in use the best storage for the club is to hang it on a wall, so before you cut the twine you may want to create a loop on the end for easy hanging.

There is something about holding the Devil's Club that brings out the wilder side of a witch. When I hold it I'm overcome with a sense that nothing can stand before me while it is in my hands. When I made mine I was jabbed on multiple occasions, and if I'm not careful holding the Club I can easily be jabbed by it again. The Devil's Club is a wild weapon that reminds me of my personal power as well as the dangers associated with witchcraft.

Switches also work well for the same purpose of beating a spirit. If you were raised in the South, you know exactly what I'm talking about. You probably already have some phantom pains on your bottom as you read this. For the Yankees reading, when a Southern momma got fed up with your back talk, she'd make you go pick a switch. A switch is a thin, green, branch used to spank a child. You learned real quick that trying to be cute by picking a thin switch just made it that much worse. Again, add a witchball to a switch and you'll be having devils beggin' you to send 'em back to hell.

Banishing Powder

A common herbal concoction in contemporary witchcraft, and one that is very useful. My witchcraft tends to be all about proactivity so having pre-made components ready for when I need to do work makes things go more smoothly. Banishing powder is the perfect example of this. Gather together herbs that you and your spirits have designated as being forceful at pushing out unwanted forces without interfering with your own spirits. Blend them in the mortar and pestle until you have a fine mix of herbs. When something Nasty is trying to mess with you, sprinkle the powder and close it out.

Sulfur and Asafetida

These two substances are ubiquitously used in banishment and exorcism[6.] The stuff is nasty, and great for getting rid of Nasties. Sulfur and asafetida were used to stop witches from working on someone, to break curses, and in older records it seems to have been intended to stop any kind of magical work[7]. So in cases where you may have gotten in over your head, use sulfur to shut it all down. If there is a particularly nasty spirit attached to someone or something, asafetida is a good go to in breaking that connection. Be mindful of their potential toxicity, especially if you are burning it in an enclosed area. Beyond its potential toxicity, both substances reeks to high heavens so keep a window open if you choose to use it. I don't combine them with any other herbs or such, it absolutely doesn't need it.

I was once talking with a Santero friend and we were discussing how our paths were similar and how they were different. We talked about banishing and we came to the conclusion that Cascarilla (powdered eggshell) and sulfur did the same jobs in our respective traditions. I told him that I envied him because eggshell doesn't have quite the same stink as sulfur thrown on a charcoal disk. A warning about Cascarilla that I always heard is that it gets rid of all spirits, including your own. My experience with sulfur and asafetida is very similar. I added a pinch to close out a work and ended up kicking back several spirits to their spirit houses. Not all the spirits were gone, and luckily the homes were right next to me, but experimenting with the sulfur let me see who would stay next to me and who would not. It may be in your best interest to do something similar.

The Keys to the Kingdom

All of these tools can be great and I recommend becoming familiar with them and plenty of other protective measures. However the most important aspect to staying safe with witchcraft is building relationships. Spirits are your in-and-out of this craft. When you have strong relationships with spirits that you can rely on, you have the keys needed to walk between the worlds.

Your familiars should be a part of almost all of your work and are especially needed when you go between the worlds. Trust in them, call them to your side. Know their strengths. Know what spirit can help you cross over, which spirit can keep you safe on the other side, and what spirit can keep your physical body safe. Knowing these details are crucial to maintaining safety.

All of these tools listed have been about keeping you safe on this side of the fence, but not on the other side. That's because when you are over there you are relying on your personal ability and that of your familiar spirit. Any other protections will come directly from your spirits.

Chapter Four

Bible and Church Magic

For all the troubles many contemporary witches have had with the church, there's some mighty fine magic taking place in those old buildings. Speaking in tongues, prophecy, visions, water cleansing, spoken charms, and the use of the most widely recognized magical book in the world: The Bible. Now church folk would never, in any lifetime, consider this magic but rather the holy miracles of the Lord. It ain't our place to argue that it is magic because for them it's not. For us witches however, there's plenty of power to be found.

Baptism

Baptism is one of the most powerful rituals in the Christian tradition, especially for someone who grew up as a Southern Baptist. In the South, baptism is a life changing full emersion event. Southern Baptist tradition dictates that only folks who choose to be baptized can go through with the ritual, unlike other traditions that Baptize at birth. When someone has, in sound body and mind, chosen to let the Christian God into your heart they are taken to a river by your church's congregation. The preacher then prays with the convert and carries the convert underwater, fully submerging them into the river. The convert is then quickly pulled out of the water, symbolically reborn in the blood of his new God. Say what you will but it's some powerful shit to go through.

Baptism also plays an important, and controversial, role in traditional witchcraft. Initiation rituals found in *The Silver Bullet* state that renouncing your baptism is a major step to becoming a witch, and this sentiment is echoed by many traditional witches. Contemporary witches and pagans often have a turbulent relationship with Christianity, often due to the very acidic relationship many churches have with people who are outside their cultural norms. Many of us were raised in these churches and had no choice but to attend services. I grew up hearing about the evils of homosexuality every Sunday for years, all the while knowing I was queer. I was constantly afraid for my soul and my safety. So the renunciation of baptism is something I understand as a witch. I understand it, but I have never renounced my baptism.

My baptism was an important marker for me and also shifted a change for me magically. I was baptized shortly after I started practicing witchcraft on the exact date of my 13th birthday. I practiced as a Christian witch and saw no friction in my personal practice, even if I knew it would cause friction for others. I was gifted a small pocket bible, that contained just the book of Psalms, as a baptism present and this became my spell book. I had framed photos of Jesus on my "altar" that I petitioned to the same way my Wiccan friends would petition Diana or Pan. I viewed my baptism as a rite of passage that gave me and my craft even more power. I eventually abandoned all aspects of Christianity because I was continually told by other witches that I simply could not be both Christian and a witch. As an adult, although I certainly do not identify as Christian, I know that Christian witches are our ancestors in very real ways. Those who were accused of witchcraft were often on a spectrum of Christianity from devout to casual. These accused witches also often admitted to using God's name in their work, a large indicator that they were more likely folk healers than witches. Folk healer or witch, either way they were accused and recorded as witches who we now draw our craft from. And they were Christian.

For me, keeping my baptism is a testament to my word. I chose to be baptized as a true believer, and when I did this I was a true believer. Although I no longer am, I acknowledge that at one time it was heartfelt and I saw so much joy on the faces of my family when I made that decision. I know that many of my ancestors also felt that joy. This is a complicated idea, but I am proud to have been baptized and I am proud to no longer be Christian. Regardless of what a witch chooses to do in regards to their baptism (if they ever were baptized that is) is up to them, as long as they do not feel pressured by anyone to act without truly wanting it.

Bible as Talisman

The church has some very strong convictions about the Bible. First it should be noted that almost all Southern Baptists believe the Bible to be the True Word of God- meaning that they believe it was literally written by the creator of the universe. As such, to them, to read from the Bible is to enact Gods will. This is a very empower train of thought. The bible itself is considered holy, even them free bibles in the hotels. All holy things have some kind of power to them and there are some things that came up in my childhood concerning the Bible that I consider talismanic properties. I can't vouch for the effectiveness of these charms, a couple even came from folks that were (as my aunts said to me) "a bit touched in the head" and are likely not very common place among other congregations.

A Bible under your pillow will keep away nightmares.
A Bible in your safe will keep you from having money stolen.
A Bible, held closed against someone's body while praying, can heal the sick.
Never put anything on top of the Bible
A Bible in a breast pocket can stop a bullet

The Word

In addition to the whole book being imbued with power, individual passages have certain virtues that make them useful for specific works. The book of psalms is my personal favorite and this sentiment is shared with witches and folk magic workers across the country. Psalm 68 is a doozy of a curse. Psalm 91 is a protective verse that I've used continuously since I was a child. There are also certain Psalms I always use when opening a divination session.

While there do exist books for the use of Psalms in magic I recommend just reading the book itself. It's not long at all and I always encourage witches to do their own legwork. Half the time I don't even agree with other witches on what verse is best for what kind of work, so I'd rather look it up myself. If you're really in a pickle, then Bible dip for it.

The Written Word

The Psalms (and other Books) can be used in magic by writing down the verse number, writing the verse itself, or tearing the verse straight from the book. These three methods have their uses and levels of appropriateness. If you just wanted a quick little boost of safety, then writing Psalms 91 on a piece of paper and carrying it in your pocket will be that little extra something that you needed. If you were hand making a protective sachet you may want to take the time and write a whole verse by hand to capture its full essence. If you have had continuous safety and protective issues and need something done with great force, take the page from the book and incorporate it into a protective doll. Ways you can use the written word are diverse and only limited to your own creativity.

Writing verse on the skin for last minuet boosts
Writing the verse, burning it to ash, and sprinkling on a target
Inscribing it onto an object to imbue the object with that power
Folding a verse into a square to act as a talisman

The Spoken Word

Usually verses are utilized in a combination of written and spoken. Spoken spells is one of the most popular witch tropes in fiction for a reason. Speaking something into being is powerful, and can sometimes be key to generating that kind of spine tingling sensation that reminds us that witchcraft ain't a game. The most basic use of spoken psalms is literally just saying the words to create a change. Beyond that you could say a verse as a way to focus the intent of a working.

Whisper a psalm over someone's drink to influence them.

Whisper psalms over your own drink to take in its power for yourself.

Loudly sing a psalm in your home to infuse the walls with the quality of the verse.

Use a booming voice to recite a psalm to invite you spirits into your space.

The Power of Blasphemy

Inversion of something from its proper role is an act of liminality that can imbue something with entirely new characteristics. Contemporary witches do this plenty already with the famous witch's cauldron. The contemporary witch most often uses cauldrons to contain fire which they dance around and call the Witch Father. This act of placing fire inside the cauldron rather than below changes the nature of the tool from mundane to magical. To invert the Bible is to blaspheme it, to desecrate what Christendom built. If the Bible is already imbued with its own holy power, to make it into a thing of blasphemy gives it an unhollowed kind of power. It is already common practice in some traditional witchcraft circles to end works with "Nema" an inversion of the popular Christian word "amen".

Witches signing their blood into the Book of Revelation is delightfully blasphemous, and can claim the Bibles power for themselves with this act. It is in some of the very first stories of *The Silver Bullet* that witchcraft is referred to as "the 'ligion of the Devil" and so to claim the power of Revelation with your own blood is one steeped in the folklore itself.

Often times the act of blasphemy in witchcraft involves theft from a church. It is interesting that many of the tales concerning these thefts involve the Catholic Church rather than Protestant churches. The stealing of communion wafers is a key ingredient to some rituals, as is stealing communion wine and holy water. Walking around church grounds a certain number of times, against the sun, is another of these acts of blasphemy used in curses and initiation rituals. And of course there is the classic black mass, in which the Lord's Prayer is reversed to conjure the Devil Himself.

For the discerning witch the use of the Bible and Church teachings in magic is most useful when done with one's own intuition. I could list the purpose of every Psalm and Deuteronomy verse and maybe one in every hundred use would line up with what the reader thinks. For those of us brought up in the church, we probably don't think too fondly on those experiences. I have a handful to be sure but mostly the things that stick with me are being nudged awake by my angry Mimi or being forced to sit through anti-queer hate speech after having just come out to my family. As negative as those experiences are, I try to see the useful information as well and I certainly don't want to ignore the place where my witchcraft started.

Chapter Five

Witchballs

The source of the Southern witch's curses and hexes, the witchball is one of the few tools the folklore gives an actual recipe for! However most of these ingredients are used to illustrate how horrible witches are in folklore. Some of these nasties have been kept while others have been replaced. The creation is also done with other witches and is a communal effort. This doesn't necessarily need to be a traditional coven, but just some likeminded witches to work with.

The creation of witchballs should only be done on Friday the thirteenth. Before this date the witches in attendance should, through divination and common sense, determine the ingredients and who should bring what. There is a strong importance on bringing the correct ingredients and amounts. The most crucial ingredients are the hair of each witch plucked at the end of the ritual and the wax itself to make the balls. All else can be determined by the coven, for their specific cursing needs. Some of my suggestions would be pepper powder, coffin nail rust, powdered lizard, graveyard dirt of a criminal, ground agrimony, bone dust, stinging nettle, ashes, mace, and the traditional spiders' legs. The traditional consequences for forgetting an ingredient are lashes from the Devil with a rose thorn and a decreased amount of witchballs. A witch who brought all her ingredients received 13, one who brought part received 7, and one who brought none received 3. The lashes can be replaced by some other unpleasant act, or done without completely.

Set up your double boiler and place some wax in. Each witch adds an ingredient, naming the purpose of the ingredient. Pepper to burn, graveyard dirt to bring illness, powdered lizard to bring quick results, and so on. The witches then surround the mixture, bring up the witch fire from their bellies, and gather the power of their familiars around to chant;

To this mystic myrrh
To make a witchball
I, the Witch Father, doth stir,
To place curses on one and all!

Stir the mixture so that the ingredients are not pooling together. Pour the mixture into containers, I use mini cupcake papers for portion control. Allow it to cool and semi harden. While still pliable the head of the coven takes globs of the mixture and wraps around each one a hair from a coven member (themselves included). When each ball is made they are portioned out.

Doing this with a coven not only shares power, but acts in a sense as an omen taking. The amount of balls you receive is

indicative of the limit of maleficium that should be performed in that year. This work is structured for a group, however that shouldn't stop a single individual from making these tools.

Traditionally the Witchball was thrown at the target and retrieved by the witch at a later time so as not to lose them (losing a bit of power and also risking the wrath of the Devil beating them) however in modern times going around throwing wax balls is not the most secretive way of cursing. Rather, a modern witch can and should include the witchballs in more specific cursing spells.[8]

How Witchballs can be used

Melting Roof Curse

On a hot day, toss a witchball at the roof of your targets home with a command. This is most useful for a particularly nasty neighbor a simple command of "Leave this home and never come back" will get the job done. This could also be done on the roof of a car. Should you wish to retrieve the Witchball at a later time, hide it under their doormat and hope they leave the mat in the move!

Poppet

The creation of poppets is a classic act in witchcraft. Poppets are created in three typical ways: cloth, wax, and clay. You create a doll in the image of a target, fill the contents of doll with herbs the work for the intended purpose (stinging nettle for curse work for example) and put a witchball at the dolls heart. The most essential part of a poppet is something to tie to the target such as hair, nails, or used clothes. Baptize the doll in the name of the target and set it in a place where it can do its work. Of the witchball curses this is one of the more labor intensive, but results from poppets are often quick and clearly visible.

Witch's Bridle

Essentially a cursed clothing item. In Hag Riding a witch's bridle forces the target into the shape of a horse and are ridden all night, leaving them exhausted and near death. In a modern form, the goal is to compel your target to do what you want them to. Obtain a piece of clothing that your target will wear. The witchball, depending on size, can be melted onto the lining of a shirt or pant. In a shoe you can use the witchball as a shoe polish or finish, or simply melt the ball on the inside of the shoe. Another option is to drop the witchball into a washbasin and wash the clothing with the water. The command for the witchball can be "give me a raise" for an employer, or literally any other compulsion command.

Counter Cursing

Witchballs can also be used to send a curse back against someone who has attempted to curse you. This can sometimes be complicated as each curse should be dealt with individually. If you can find the curse object placed on you then you can melt the witchball onto it and send it back to the origin. I specify using agrimony in the wax mixture because of its use in counter cursing.

Lantern

The Silver Bullet has a story titled *Jack-ma-lanterns* that gave me the idea of using the jack-o-lantern as a magical tool. The original story details jack-ma-lanterns being similar to will-o-the-wisps, leading people astray. This gave me the idea for a tool which protects a home by leading potential threats astray, or by more aggressive means if necessary. Pumpkins rot over time, and so are not ideal. However a gourd can be carved a using rotary tool to create a permanent lantern. With the lantern has been created, and the spirit of the lantern addressed and given its purpose, tea lights made of witchballs can be placed inside for house protection.

Exorcism

In the same way that witchballs could be used to evict a human from their home, they can be used to evict an unwanted spirit from your own. This could be used in combination with the Lantern as described and the Devil's Club discussed in the chapter on protection.

Healing

This is a complicated approach that is likely to be very unfamiliar to those who are used to approaching healing magic through new age perspectives. As an animist all things have spirits. Trees, rivers, and stones are things we are comfortable thinking of as enspirited. Viruses and diseases also have their own spirits and can be interacted with as spirits. Some may choose to bargain with these spirits or to have them transfer to another vessel. Both of these are valid in their own right, however with a witchball healing can be done more like an exorcism. The spirit can be forced out by siccing the witchball on it, having the sickness spirit be torn apart so that the virus no longer has anything to keep it going. Essentially you are healing the person by cursing the sickness. This is not something I recommend to be tried lightly, but it is a possible approach. As always, witchcraft is not a replacement for appropriate physical and mental health treatment.

Chapter Six

The Cost of Cursing

The job of the witch in folklore is to curse. However in most stories that doesn't seem to end well for the witch. Most witches get foiled by the lay man, but every once in a while a witch meets her match from another magical practitioner. Conjurers, Pellars, and Cunning Folk are all known for their talent to undo witchcraft. Folkloric witches straddle these lines comfortably. We don't mind undoing a curse just as fast as we'd cast it. More than once in folktales the lines between folk magical practitioners and witches are blurred. As folkloric witches we keep this tradition alive.

Counter cursing works differently from other forms of magic involving people. In curse work attaining someone's personal concerns gives a spell the curse a lot of power. Cursing someone connects the witch to the person, meaning that there is no need for personal concerns of the witch themselves to send it back. When you as a witch send a curse you run the risk of having a counter curse used. Curses should be thought through for a number of reasons, and the risk of counter cursing is one of them.

Counter cursing is often very detailed in folklore, often because folklore acts as a tool to teach some kind of a lesson. The lesson in this case being "one day you'll piss off a witch and you better know what to do about it." So here you'll find some tailored counter cursing spells drawn from the folklore.

To harm a witch who has cursed you, and undo the curse in the process, you first locate whatever has been cursed. If it's cattle or an individual, clip some of that person's hair and burn it with a pinch of sulfur. If it's dairy, you take the milk or butter and heat it in a pan. You then violently whip the milk with a Devil's Club. This will reverse the hex and send the damage back on the one who sent it to you. The key elements to take away here is the influence of fire and thorns on the cursed item.

If you have been having some minor bad luck and think someone may have given you the evil eye you can try the following to remove it. Speak the names of the Holy Trinity, put your pockets inside out, wrap a piece of silver and place it on your person, or draw a ring around yourself. Flipping pockets is an old folk custom to undo the illusionary influence of Good Neighbors in Ireland and Scotland.

To prevent something from being witched you can put brass in it somehow. Brass has the curious property of being immune to witchcraft and the brass itself does not need to be large. A brass screw was said to prevent guns from being witched.

Using a witch bottle to send a curse back to its sender: Put nail clippings, hair, urine, and straight pins into a bottle. Originally, place it under a burning fire and light three white candles in the name of the Father, Son, and Holy Ghost. Don't allow anyone to enter the home for three days following. This is to ensure that the witch does not come back to re-curse the family.

To prevent witches or nasty spirits from entering a home place of bowl of rice or any grain by the front door. In folklore witches and spirits are compelled to count anything placed in front of them. This supposedly keeps the intruder trapped outside until the sun rises and sends the spirit back to where it came from.

If a witch is preventing you from moving forward, use divination to determine who the witch is. For this kind of naming divination you may choose to do a bible and key approach. Once determined either obtain an image of the witch or make one. If the name cannot be determined it is best to make a clay doll. At either a crossroads or well driven dirt road dig a small grave for the image. Bury it with ceremony and drive over the grave never looking back. If the witch has been particularly atrocious you may create multiple graves across a large area to prevent the witch from finding you.

To break the magical influence of a witch over you using the witchball take your witchball and roll it in a mix of boar hair (or other aggressive animal), sulfur, asafetida, and molasses. Go to a young tree (folklore specifies a sapling) who's spirit knows you. Speak to it, get permission to peel sizable bark. Draw an image of the witch, borrowing the tree spirits help in assuring the image connects with the witch. Lob the witchball, wrapped in the mixture, at the image. Make sure that the bark is held in such a way that being hit by the witchball will damage it. Leave the place without turning back.

To make a witch's power decay get a slab of meat, tie string around the slab and at exactly midnight hang it in a secluded area where it will not be disturbed. Name the meat for the witch who has cursed you and command the witch's power to decay as the meat does. Variation: take the meat to a wooded area, and as the animals tear it to pieces over time so will the witches' power be eaten and divided.

In the most extreme cases of a witch bothering you, there is an option to kill a witch's power. Stories often tell us that witches die when they've been countered, but one story gives an insight that makes a bit more sense to this. In *Butter, Witches, and Thorns* a woman tells us that you don't literally kill the witch but rather "her power to witch will be dead, and she cain't never do you no more devilment"[9]. Take your Devil's Club if you believe yourself to have been cursed. If your home has been cursed get some dirt from your yard and mix it with the ashes of your own hair, and beat it mercilessly with the Devil's Club. This will kill a witch's influence over you so long as you do not allow the witch to take anything from you. This should also exist as a warning, that should you be counter cursed then you may take a hit to your own personal power. Other sorted counter curses and bits of advice are,

Draw a ring around yourself
In a fire throw henbane, nightshade, sulfur, copperas
Written charms worn around the neck
While counter cursing, do not allow anyone into your home and tell
  no one that you have done a counter curse

Preventing Counter Curses

If you have sent a curse to someone you run the risk of counter curses. Not as frequently as would have been 70 years ago when rural folks believed in witches a bit more, but it is still a risk. We should also not assume that all counter curses will be in spell form, the church does well with protecting their flock with their exorcisms and such. There are some practical and magical efforts that you can go to that would help avoid the costs of cursing.

Curse Wisely. Not every situation warrants a curse. If you're cursing every sonovabitch who cuts you off in traffic, you are increasing your odds of counter cursing simply by creating more opportunity for the counter curses to take place. Attempting to curse another magical practitioner is a massive risk compared to cursing an average Joe racist neighbor or harmful ex. On more than one occasion magical practitioners have gone back and forth for years at a time in what's commonly called a "witch war" and is normally a waste of time and energy.

Everyone has their personal ethics about cursing, for me cursing normally takes the form of last resort. It has to be a really calculated move to get to the point where a curse happens and personally only when someone's safety or security is in jeopardy.

Set limits. Don't allow a curse to go on till the end of days. Give the curse and your spirits a limit. Say "they are cursed until they can no longer harm me" or "until they give me back the money they owe me" whatever it is just place a cut off for it. Curses take a lot of effort on your part and your spirits part, so set boundaries.

Enlist the help of spirits. This goes without saying, but if you're the only one working a curse then you're the only target for a counter curse. Spiritual assistance spreads the love, and can potentially hide you completely from counter measures.

Use witchballs. When made well, and guided by spirits, the effects of a witchball is difficult to undo. This may be for a number of reasons for instance the division of influence on the witchball. These witchballs are made with other witches, counter curses are intended to send a curse back to the caster. If the counter curse doesn't have an exact target to send back to, it dissipates. Witchballs are also inherently powerful tools, imbued with the influences of other witches and the Witch Father himself. That kind of kick takes more than inside-out pockets to undo.

Chapter Seven

Initiation by Spirit in the American South

Initiation is often the single defining moment of a witch's life. It is the death of the old self and birth of the new one, a person who has taken life into their own hands. This was true in the folklore, and is true today. Contemporary witchcraft religions are by-and-large initiation based and strongly emphasize the death and rebirth of the initiate. These religions are often called "Red Thread" traditions by contemporary practitioners. Red Thread means that the tradition is something passed down person to person, that you can meet another person of the same lineage and be assured that your teachings are almost identical. These initiations can only be done by other individuals who have already undergone initiations into the religion or tradition. These are the initiations that a contemporary witch reading this book is likely to be the most familiar with. What we see in the folklore is something entirely different.

In folklore what we find follows a trend. The story of Jonas Dodson helps illustrate how initiation often plays out for the Southern witch. Jonas was the son of a preacher who fell in love with a witch. Jonas decided he wanted to become a witch himself, and his lover took him to the oldest witch in her clan. This old witch told Jonas that despite her experience and talents in witchcraft, she cannot make him into a witch. It's not that she doesn't want to make Jonas a witch, but rather no person can make another a witch. She communes with the spirit who made her a witch, and then teaches Jonas how to conduct a ritual that will summon this spirit and initiate him into witchcraft. The ritual Jonas conducts calls to the Devil Himself on a mountaintop, while other rituals call a black dog at a riverbed or an old man at the crossroads. These spirits hold the traditions of witchcraft and they decide who receives initiation.

This kind of spirit initiation is what this book will present the tools for. Rituals here are signals to spirits that you are seeking initiation, and does not guarantee the spirits will reciprocate. This kind of initiation by spirit is called "White Thread". This tradition does not make any claims of authenticity over other approaches and claims no ancient history. It is inherently modern, with generations old roots. White thread initiation is a direct transmission of power from spirit to mortal. No middle man, very little must-dos, and only one person to impress is the spirit. Following in the footsteps of folklore, I've put together rituals that focus on the making of a witch. Initiation essentially means beginnings. I do not encourage the reader to dive head first into the rituals however. I encourage the reader to read, digest, and dissect the information in this book before attempting anything within. Many of these practices do not require any initiation, either white or red thread. Use this book as a tool to make the most informed decisions for yourself.

You will live life with many initiations, spiritual and mundane. Some will be formal, some will be as casual as a hand shake- but they are all impactful. That is why I have included some elements that are not found in the folklore. There are a series of rituals designed to call to a particular entity and get to know them. I will refer to this entity as The Witch Father. In folklore his most common name is the Devil but he is also called the Black Woodsman or Old Scratch. This is the spirit who led me through these rituals, and who this book is dedicated to. Of all the lessons I learned along this winding road, the most crucial for me is that everything boils down to informing yourself as much as possible and holding yourself accountable to your actions. If you do not have these principals then it is likely that this approach will not be of the most use to you. It makes no difference to me if it is The Black Woodsman who you meet, or a local spirit, or an ancestral spirit. Rest assured that I won't be over your shoulder saying what you're doing is wrong. Take this experience and do what is best for your spirits and yourself. Any missteps, any frustrations, any excitement or ecstasy is of your own making. Revel in that.

Initiation is a death. Something in you has to die in order to be initiated, to be given the information or power these spirits have. Sometimes initiation can result in physical illness, life changing events, job losses, or emotional upheaval. This is not meant to scare the reader, just inform that these rituals are intended to help signal to the spirits that you are ready to be initiated, to be torn apart and put back together. This is a cross cultural experience that can be read about among not just witches confessions, but also the occurrence of what anthropologist term "shamanic death" that occurs in some indigenous religious traditions. The rituals do not guarantee that you will experience this, but any successful initiation comes at a cost.

On the Experience and Detriment of Spirit Initiation

Writing about initiation is difficult, especially in these terms. The rituals included are initiatory in that they are formal beginnings on a path, however they are not the initiations themselves. This can be confusing, but so is most of witchcraft. Initiation comes from spirits, and so what the spirits put you through is going to be different for each person. It's not something that I feel should be rushed into. It is incredibly personal and involves being torn apart. I have become incredibly sick from initiations, and although it ended up opening major doors for me it closed others.

The initiation with my spirits was about making a choice. At the time I was between several different magical paths and being an idealist I wanted to a part of all of them equally. The spirits however made it apparent that it wasn't going to happen that way for me. I became sick, I left my body. I was eaten. Spirits stood before me and told me they could help me, but I could only take one hand outstretched to me. I chose, and the other spirits left. I got better, and I was changed. Shortly after this experience I left the coven I had been training in, moved far from where I had been practicing, and away from the spiritual houses that I had begun to work in. I began working alone for the first time in years. I went back to practices I had abandoned because I had been told "real witches don't use the Bible" or that to do magic I needed rare herbs from distant apothecaries.

My initiation involved sickness, loss of relationships, and closing of doors. It also led to union with my spirits, a deep understanding of my roots, and an immediacy in my magic. It also wasn't my last initiation.

In the process of creating this book, I crafted many rituals to come to terms with how folklore could inform my practice. Conducting the Killing the Moon ritual marked a period of intense life changes. I changed jobs and had health problems come and go for a period of a year. An opportunity for a high paying job with wonderful benefits appeared, and ended up being one of the most detrimental contributions to my health that I had ever experienced. About a year after the ritual had been done things started to come to a head. I quit my well-paying job and risked unemployment to improve my health. When I did this, my life improved drastically. I got a new job that completely changed my outlook on how a career should feel.

It's hard to pin down whether or not these things resulted from the spirit initiation or not. I believe that by conducting the ritual I firmly said to the Witch Father, "I am ready to move forward in my craft in a way that I have never done before". I believe that the Witch Father agreed with me. In addition to all of that, I was presented with hundreds of chances where witchcraft became necessary to solve problems. I had never needed witchcraft to really solve problems before then, and that was what this initiation was about for me. These rituals are about fully embracing what it means to be a witch. That means knowing how to make the call on when to use magic. That also means that the magic has to work. Every time.

I firmly believe that the omens exist for a reason, and that the spirits will often times chose not to initiate if someone is not ready. But I can't possibly guarantee that. The spirits can take advantage of you, or simply give you a swift kick in the ass for asking too early. I had been practicing for ten years when I did these rituals, and I think that was why the spirits agreed it was time.

This is not to scare anyone by any means, but I do want to illustrate that initiation is life changing. You can practice damn near everything in this book without ever doing the Killing the Moon ritual. The Bone doesn't require it, and the Silver Bullet isn't the only protective talisman out there. I don't think it's a terrible path to take by any means, I just want the reader to know full well what spirit initiation looks like and what it can entail. I also included my first initiatory experience to illustrate that you can be initiated without ever asking for it, and that the experience can be unpleasant. In the long run the life changes I experienced exposed the toxic parts of my life, and showed me how to heal. It taught me how to make my witchcraft that much more powerful, and it taught me that I should never make choices based on money.

Given that initiation is not necessary to practice magic and that initiation can be a horrible experience, why would anyone want to do it? Especially back when being a witch was grounds for being shunned or killed? I often turn to the story of Jonas Dodson when thinking about initiation. Jonas was the son of a preacher in the Appalachian mountain range. His father had every intention of Jonas growing up and taking over as a preacher. However Jonas fell in love with a Melungeon woman who his father disapproved of. This woman also happened to be a witch, and Jonas had decided he also wanted to be a witch.

Jonas left his family, abandoned his legacy, and endured three years of failed initiations to finally become a witch. When I read his story and think back on my own experience with the church and having family reject me because of who I loved, something becomes clear. Through my eyes, I can see how Jonas may have felt betrayed by his family and his faith. The world of faith put him at someone else's mercy, it stripped him of autonomy. Witchcraft is the opposite of this, it places all of your actions at your feet and makes you responsible for them. Witchcraft, I'd argue, is all about autonomy.

The bond of initiation is like a marriage. Marriage is not necessary to show your love to someone, and sometimes it makes things that much more messy. Still it is a powerful bond that when done well and maintained in a healthy way can bring people together for the long haul. Initiation brings you closer to your spirits, it shows you how you can rely on each other, and how to teach each other in ways that no one else can. Initiation creates a family of spirits. I think what Jonas saw was that the Devil and the Melungeon's took care of their own in the way a man of God never did for him.

Power

The concept of power in witchcraft is one that is highly debated. There are those who view power as being clarity in knowledge, or as universal love for others. Traditional views of power found in witchcraft are a little more on-the-nose than that. Power is defined by how you can impact the world around you through witchcraft, or by your communication with spirits who can work on your behalf. Folkloric witches were known to be given power in the form of either a tool or a familiar. Sometimes, several familiars would build up a witch's ability to impact the world and those around them.

The view of power presented here is much the same, with a few other questions thrown in. How many familiars can a witch tend to and work with at a given time? How clearly can a witch discern when magic is needed and when it is not? How immediate are results from a given working? None of these questions can be answered by anyone other than the witch themselves. With this view, power is not a tool to hold over the heads of others. Power is the ability to discern, observe, act, and change what surrounds you. Observation has been covered with divination and omen watching. Discernment is also tied with divination, and will be mentioned often when talking about self-accountability. Action is personal, this is tied to common sense and timing, things that no book could ever teach. Finally we come to changing the desired outcome. This can be accumulated through the assistance of the Witch Father, tools, and familiar spirits.

There are two popular concepts related to power and witchcraft through most traditional circles. Witch Blood and Witch Fire. Witch Blood is essentially the idea that certain people are born with the ability to do witchcraft through their lineage, and that those without Witch Blood are at a disadvantage in terms of practicing witchcraft. Witch Fire is the concept that within a witch there is a pool of power, wild and sometimes uncontrollable, that can either be gifted by spirits or something the witch is born with. I find the concept of the Witch Fire to be much more in line with my experiences of spirit work and personal dedication. I also like the idea that while witchcraft may not be for everyone it is possible through dedication to form bonds with spirits who can bring you power. This to me emphasizes the importance of work within the craft, and maintaining connections to those who help you.

Witch Fire is often felt as a literal heat within the body. Something that causes the body to move, to shake, to dance. Letting the Witch Fire move through you can seem almost like possession, an abandonment of civility. The fire changes you from within and brings you closer to the wilderness, the ferocity of the land and the ferocity within yourself. To let the fire burn within you is to accept the danger and ecstasy of witchcraft. This is what makes witchcraft so different from other forms of magic. It is not just correct methods, or petitions to spirits that make changes, but the assumption of wild fire from inside of you that changes the world around you. It is not possible to light the fire without being changed.

Meeting at the Crossroads

Those who have never met the Witch Father should go to the crossroads at midnight, a liminal time when cars are unlikely to be on the road. This is a simple rite of introduction. Bring with you a small offering of whiskey or beer. Announce yourself to the Witch Father by whatever name you call him. Leave the offering and state why you wish to become acquainted with him. Be honest; speak plainly and respectfully about why you are there. Stay for a time, meditate, and watch for omens. Don't expect to see a full manifestation of the Man in Black, be open to smaller omens such as barking dogs or suddenly snapping twigs. After you have felt the presence of the Witch Father and communicated your wants and needs, return home never looking back.

Repeat this rite several times in order to become acquainted with the Witch Father, try and see if a partnership is the best thing for you. Allow him to teach you personal spells and rituals not found elsewhere, take advice on personal issues, kick back and enjoy your offerings with him. The purpose of the following rituals is to gain blessings, partnerships, and power but they start here at the crossroads. The more time you spend at the crossroads, the more successful these later rituals become.

After you've grown accustomed to meeting at the crossroads, consider holding crossroads rituals in your magical space. Draw a four armed cross on the ground in corn meal or chalk and invite the Witch Father to join you. Create a crossroads and be in the presence of the Witch Father on your own turf.

The Black Bible and Other Magical Books

Grimoires are instructional books of magic that have likely existed as long as writing itself has. These books were known to be owned by cunning men throughout Europe and even if a cunning man was illiterate, just the ownership of these books were thought to bring power and certain spirits to the cunning man[10.] These books are heavily associated with conjuration, the summoning of spirits, but also includes spells and rituals for various goals. In America some of these grimoires made their way over, and is particularly noted in the powwow traditions among the Pennsylvania Dutch[11.] The two books that make the most frequent appearances in American witch lore are The Devil's Book and the Holy Bible.

The Devil's Book is described as a book owned by the Devil that a witch signs her name into, usually in the witch's own blood. This created a binding pact between the Devil and the witch, making the witch subservient to the Devil while granting the witch power. This typically happened during a witch's first visit with the Devil and was an accessory element to an overall initiatory experience. The initiations explored herein do include pacts, but not one of subservience. There is also no physical, human manifestation of the Witch father that we expect to appear during the ritual. So the purpose of this book changes, but still plays a role.

The Holy Bible can sometimes take the place of the Devil's Book in many ways. In tales found in the *The Silver Bullet* the witch signed her name in the Book of Revelation specifically rather than an unnamed Devil's Book. Many times the Bible itself acts as a grimoire. Growing up in the South many of the older folks in church would prescribe certain Bible passages to help ailments. Of course this was never thought of as magic, this was just reading the Word of God. I was told by some of these folks, who knew I was interested in witchcraft growing up, that I should sleep with my Bible to ward off the Devil.

Growing up I often hid my witchcraft through the use of the Bible. I did in fact sleep with my bible to ward off evil spirits, and I also read Psalm 91 for protection and prayed over objects to carry the power of the Psalms. The book of Psalms has a particularly long magical history in both America and Europe, and many grimoires mention the use of Psalms in conjuration work.

The contemporary witch may use these ideas in a number of different ways. The Bible can be used as both a spell book and talisman. A blank book can be used to write down the names of familiars, ancestors, and oaths you may have taken. This book of spirits should be set aside so that it does not constantly get filled with other notes and you are not forced to flip through pages of notes to find needed contact information of a certain spirit. And last, a personal grimoire filled with the witches experiences.

Contemporary witches will be most familiar with the concept of a magical journal of sorts where they can track spells, jot ideas, and compose recipes in. Recording your experiences is essential to reflecting on them and being able to keep track of progress. Most contemporary witches are familiar with this process and have some kind of record of their magical progress. It is highly recommended that you start writing as soon as you begin making contact at the crossroads. Starting to write that early on gives you a record that you can always go back to. Initiation can be a blurry experience and your memory might not always be reliable during this time so a written record can be very helpful.

Before the Rite of Killing the Moon

This ritual is one of cleansing and initiation. If the omens are right for you, this ritual will do more than reorient you to a magical worldview. This is meant to begin the process of spiritual initiation, to put the White Thread into your hands. Initiations can be hard, they can even invoke hardships on you. With spirit initiation can also come major life changes, spirit sickness, and all around unpleasantness. This is a part of the death of the old life and beginning of a new life as a witch. Not everyone will have the same experience. Not everyone will feel the need to approach this ritual at all. If the Witch Father has lead you to this point, know that any good initiation is a life changing one.

In this ritual another entity is mention, The Witch Mother. In the original story, the moon is not personified in anyway. Contemporary witches however have a huge reverence for the moon and consider it the mother of witches. In respect for this entity and acknowledging the role of the moon in witchcraft there are calls to the Witch Mother. In Cory Hutcherson's article *Killing the Moon* he makes reference to the whole ritual as "Celestial Sacrifice" a concept that has greatly influence this work[12]. The concepts boils down to a mirroring between the witch and the moon, the Witch Mother. The visual omen of the bloody moon is a sign that part of the witch has been replaced with the Witch Mothers blood, taking the witch one step closer to the wild.

The original story found in *The Silver Bullet* contains some themes that have been changed in this adaptation. For instance I do not include the renunciation of my Baptism, I also utilize another practice known as Moon Raking, and I replace the silver bullet with another piece of silver. I consider my Baptism to be a part of my ancestral traditions, much like my witchcraft. As such the renunciation is not something I find necessary, and is not included. The use of moon raking[13] is done to mitigate the throwing or shooting of bullets into the air, something that is dangerous even by witchcraft standards. The replacement of the silver bullet with a piece of silver is done because finding a silver bullet is rather difficult and cost much more than using silver already owned by the witch. I used a silver ring because that was what worked for me and my relationship with the Witch Father. What I write below is meant to be framed as a bare bones approach, one that gives the template and allows for your personal spiritual relationship to changes as needed. Keep that in mind throughout the book and its rituals.

I will continue to refer to the central ritual tool as the Silver Bullet, but keep in mind it does not have to be a literal silver bullet. This item can, through this ritual, become a symbol of your relationship with the Witch Father but more importantly will become a talisman representing yourself and directing your strength.

Killing the Moon

For thirteen days go to a river or creek at sunrise, bringing your silver with you. Wash your silver in the river, saying "Wash me clean of the grime of the world as this bullet is of grease." This ritual cleansing will free you of the binds of your daily life, creating time for your spirits. It is also a ritual cleansing of oaths you may have taken and wish to clean yourself of. Finally, this act is known to attract the attention of the Witch Father. The repetition of this ritual is a show of dedication to the crooked path and to your spirit work. On the thirteenth night, take a bowl to catch the moon in. Catching the moon means that the moon is clearly reflected in the water. Or find where the moon is clearly visible on the surface of the river. Take your silver and say a prayer over it.

As the Witch Mother dies by this bullet
And her blood fills the sky
May it fall onto me and fill me
With her power as she is reborn eternal

Drop or hurl the bullet into the water and as the water ripples, visualize the moon bleeding and filling the sky. Maintain vigil for a time awaiting for any immediate omens that may occur, particularly in regards to the sky. Shooting stars or sudden anomalous weather changes can be taken for particularly strong omens. Animal sounds and appearances may also be good signs.

Should nothing happen immediately hold a vigil for the next thirteen days at both sunrise and moonrise, if either celestial body appear to be bleeding the ritual has succeeded. If not, repeat the ritual on the next full moon.

If the omens have shown to be true, place one hand on your head and the other on your foot. Traditionally one offers all that is betwixt their hands to the Witch Father. I say that you should own yourself, and must own yourself before any such offer can be made. In my years of practice I have dedicated myself to the Witch Father in many ways, but never a blind offer of my soul.

All that lies betwixt my hands
filled to the brim with power

All that lies betwixt my hands
belong to myself and my own power

All that lies betwixt my hands
grows by the blessings of the Powers

After the Rite

This ritual is not complicated, but it does create many changes. It opens a door inside the witch that allows for power to enter. This power effects the witch and the tools used throughout the ritual. The silver bullet in particular becomes an extension of the witch that one should take particular care of. Many folktales tell of a witch losing a magical item, only to have it used against them. This is a protective amulet as well as a power based talisman. It is something that keeps you protected from the evil eye, opens you to spirit communication, and quickens your magical growth.

If the bullet cannot be kept on the witch constantly, put it in a place of importance such as an altar. As this ritual is intended to be a personal encounter with powerful forces, the bullet may become something entirely different for you than what it is for me. It may become a spirit home for a familiar, a direct line to the Witch Father, or something I can't even conceive of. Be open to its development as well as your own. Alternatively the silver bullet may be used as it was originally intended, to be thrown and never picked up again. In this case the silver becomes and offering to the spirits themselves.

The water used in the original story is specifically a river running in the opposite direction of the suns course. Where I live in Southwest Florida, there are no rivers that run this way. I live in an area that made it almost impossible to get to any body of water every single morning for this cleansing. However, Florida is known for its flash thunderstorms. Every morning it just so happened that a storm was brewing on my way to work. My bullet was a silver ring. Every morning I held my hand out the window of my car on my way to work and prayed "Wash me clean of the grime of the world as this bullet is of grease" while the rain water washed over me. Adapt this to your local area.

The shortest amount of time this ritual should take is thirteen days. However it could take months if the omens are not clear. If you feel disheartened or let down because the omens have not occurred, remember the story of Jonas Dodson, our Mighty Dead Ancestor. Jonas was the son of Reverend Hiriam Dodson and came from a long line of preachers. It took Jonas three years' worth of moon killing (in his case sun killing) before he found a familiar waiting for him at home. The witch that taught him explained that after years of his family trying to stop the Devil, it took a lot of time for the Devil to truly trust him. Jonas eventually lived to an old age and became an accomplished and "wicked conjure man". The ritual takes time, and maybe the repetition is a part of the Witch Father's plan to make you that much more powerful. Be patient and watch the omens.

The Conjure Bone

This is one of the few highly important tools listed in this book, right alongside the Black Book. The Conjure Bone is essentially a talisman of power and luck, something that builds itself up and serves a unique purpose for the witch. It is something that collects its strength through its connection with the witch and the witch's familiars. The more times the witch uses it, the more effective its ability to create desired effects. The Bones purpose can change for each individual, but more or less it acts as the bastion of the power we use.

I would compare the bone to something akin to a stang, in that it is an altar unto itself. The Bone is a marker of all that makes a particular witch the kind of witch they are. It grows with the witch in a way other tools do not. It is an extension of the witch's spirit, and occasionally appears to be its own spirit. It is protective, receptive, and can direct a witch's will. I'm not one to talk about the mysteries of witchcraft often, but I would in consider this one of them. Unless you have this kind of talisman it can be very difficult to explain.

Many modern witchcraft traditions use the phrase "mystery" to refer to something that is closed off to outsiders. Often times that phrase is used colloquially in order to show superiority over another practitioner; essentially stating that one is better than the other because they have "learned the true mysteries". However for the folk witch a mystery means much more simply something that cannot be explained without experiencing it first. It is not used to create a sense of superiority, but rather to illustrate the experiential nature of folkloric witchcraft.

This tool does of course come with both pros and cons. A pro is that over time a witch may find themselves needing less tools because the bone grows to encompass many purposes. A con is that much of a witch's power will begin to reside in the bone, meaning that to lose it can be dire to a witch's practice. It won't end their career as a witch, but could certainly be a blow to the accumulated work put in.

Another major pro is that a witch with this talisman only

really needs that one talisman. In 2017 a horrific hurricane came through Southwest Florida and was slated to destroy my neighborhood due to storm surge. I had an entire room dedicated to my craft, and I immediately knew that only one thing needed to be saved- the bone. Everything else in the room was in some way already touched by the bone, so I didn't have to take the time to decide what needed to be taken with me. I wasn't bound by extensive ritual tools, I had one thing that was important knowing everything else could be replaced. In reality of course, the bone can also be replaced, but the point is that when push comes to shove no other tool matches up to the bone in versatility.

The story of how the bone is attained is horrific; to become a witch you catch a black cat, take it down to the river, boil it, and then wash the bones in the river till the Devil comes. When he appears the bone you are holding at that time becomes your talisman. Another method is to actually scratch open the cats stomach beforehand. The fact that there are multiple ways to gain the bone in even the same story encouraged me to think that you don't need animal abuse to be inspired by the tale.[14]

The ritual for the bone found in the folklore includes many aspects that I have removed. Folklore is inspiration, not gospel. One rule that should be maintained from folklore is that should someone steal your Conjure Bone, you are going to be highly exposed. Witches in folklore always have a weak spot, and losing the Conjure Bone is a huge one. Should you lose it, according to the folklore, you lose your magical power. If it is stolen, someone could do great harm to you. I hold true to this, mostly because the bone is fed with your own blood and power making it a personal concern to be used against you. Of course some Conjure Bones have a mind of their own and may not take kindly to being turned against you, but it's better to be safe than sorry.

For the purpose of this book the Conjure Bone will be used as the central object of power, however each witch will find their own object of power that may or may not be a bone. For witches who primarily work with the dead, animals, or other spirits then bones are the most likely candidate. However stones and roots are equally as likely and the Witch Father (or your familiar) may give you reasons as to why you have something else. There is at least one instance of a magic worker in the Appalachian mountain range using a stone as an object of power. This magic worker is discussed in the ethnography *Signs, Cures, and Witchery* by Gerald C. Milnes. The woman in the book had a stone that she always kept on her mantel and would turn clockwise to bring her money[15.] These kinds of specifics can't be taught in a book, but by reading through these I hope that the reader can discern an approach that works.

This ritual is by no means unique to *The Silver Bullet* and in fact was widely popular in folk magic throughout America and Europe. The source of the ritual is attributed to St. Cyprian in a Portuguese grimoire, however in America it has been popularized through hoodoo. In addition there are other animal bone rituals that are very similar, notably the Toad Bone ritual in which a toad is crucified and eaten alive by ants to reveal the magical bone. The name of the bone being *Conjure* is interesting to note because the word is heavily associated with African American folk magic and European Cunning Craft.

This ritual is however its own beast and is vastly different from the source material. Namely the method in which the bone is found. Boiling a cat alive is simply something that doesn't sit well with me and I'd venture to say most folks wouldn't stand for it either. Because the bone in this new ritual is found from an already dead animal, or an animal killed for sustenance, the nature of the ritual changes as well. Not to mention other factors such as who the practitioner is, where they are located, and at what point in history they exist. All of these factors make the ritual listed here something very different, yet still at the heart of what witchcraft accomplishes. Witchcraft is mediating between the dead and the living, putting spirits to rest, and eliciting the assistance of animal's spirits to call the Witch Father to our side.

Rite of the Rescued Animal

Note that this ritual involves a real bone, finding an animal carcass, preparing it, and laying its spirit to rest. If you are a hunter, you can switch this around and change the ritual to fit that lifestyle. If you slaughter your own livestock, that as well can be powerful as you will literally be using the entire animal rather than letting anything go to waste. The most important factor in this is that you are not killing an animal *for* this purpose. The original tale is brutal in its treatment of a black cat. I have tailored this ritual to be a search for roadkill, contacting the animal's spirit, and laying its remains in a dignified burial.

Start by contacting the Witch Father. State that you wish to create the Conjure Bone to assist you in your craft and form a stronger bond between yourself and the Witch Father - or for whatever purpose it is that you may want to make one. Just be honest either way. Confirm through omens or divination that the Witch Father is present. A good sign is normally a prickling of your scalp or getting goose skin. Once you have that confirmation, state your intention to search for an animal that has been struck on the road to serve as the conjure bone.

Now it's your job to keep your eyes open and your car prepared. You could go on long trips to search for roadkill, which may or may not be successful depending on how rurally you live. I suggest just allowing this to be an open invitation because this may take time and that's okay! Depending on the state of the animal discovered it may be possible to save several other parts (the fur, feathers, claws, teeth) to use as other ritual tools at a later time. If for whatever reason (like if you don't have a truck to throw the animal in) your final option would be to either buy a selection of animal bones, or to save chicken bones from your next cook out. You may already have a suitable bone that has no existing work done to it, this could also be acceptable. Conduct a funeral for the animal. Honor the animal with libations and offerings and treat it like royalty. Any time an animal death is involved in out Craft, they must be treated like Gods-On-Earth regardless of whether or not we have done the killing. Ask the spirit for its permission to use its remains in your rite, stating who you are and what work it is that you do. Try and take into account that this animal may not be friendly towards humans, rightfully so in the case of roadkill, and may be hesitant to help. If the offerings and presence of your spirits aren't enough to convince the spirit to assist you there are two options moving forward. You can either bury the body and continue the search or conduct a ritual of cutting ties. Both of these approaches will empower the full scope of the working but in different ways. Use your discretion and best judgment.

Down by the River

Take the bones or carcass down to the river (or marked sacred place) and set up your boiling pot. Boil any flesh off. Strain the contents (be prepared for the smell) and wait for the bones to cool. Then begin hand washing the bones in the stream, never taking your eyes off the mouth of the stream. If you have cleaned the bone and the Witch Father has not appeared, let the bone float in the water and grab the next. When the Witch Father appears hold onto the bone in your hand and dump the remains into the stream. This is your Conjure Bone, a lucky talisman and the reservoir of your power.

Return to your camp or home never looking back, with the exception of rear view mirrors[16]. Depending on the fragility of the bone you may take several approaches to utilizing its properties. A sturdy bone (like a leg bone from a mammal) may be carried in a pocket or put under a pillow with no concerns to it breaking. A particularly small bone may be placed in a bottle necklace. A fragile but larger bone may be placed in a sacred box or coffin like you would a mandrake root. Be mindful of what works for you. The bone should be fed the witch's own blood to empower it. How one uses it specifically is dependent on the work they conduct and the type of bone. For instance if you went the coffin route, place it on your altar and go before it like you would a sacred relic, touching it to receive its blessing and covering it when not in use. If it's in a bottle it can be hung around a bed post for flight.

A use for the bone that is obvious from the name, but not talked about in the lore, is spirit conjuration. The bone is something liminal, dead but kept alive through reverence and magic. Its liminal nature with the mixture of blood and power make its use in creating thin places very effective.

The finished tool is a sign of authority among spirits, but is to be kept a secret from other people. The bones' nature is almost an ongoing spell, and like all spells it is empowered by secrecy. If you find yourself unlucky enough to have lost or broken your Conjure Bone consult your divination immediately.

Chapter Eight

Making the Crossroads

There will be times when you are unable to go to a crossroads physically in order to make magic. Most contemporary witchcraft traditions circumvent this by creating a kind of temporary sacred space. The Wiccan circle is immediately recognizable, and the Traditional Craft Compass is another variation on the same idea. In our practice there is much less emphasis on sacred space, and more of an emphasis on places of power and thin places. Places where power is easily raised, tapped into, and molded. Thin places are places in which the boundary between our spirits and our bodies are thinner and easier to navigate, making spirit flight or conjuration easier. Ideally these would be places outside of the home where we can work openly and mingled with our local spirits. Realistically most witches will do the majority of their work in their home at a dedicated space.

A work space, magic room, or altar will not be filled with power right away. It takes time to build power on something. I do not utilize circles in my work because on a spiritual level these circles involve keeping out a lot of influences and invoking many spirits that tend to play very little roles in the work or the witch's life. Rather than cast circles, I have found it more fitting to create a crossroad to work on. We have already gone to the crossroads several times, now we are creating an in-home crossroads that can be opened and closed as needed.

On the subject of spiritual protection, many will point to the circle as inherently necessary in magic because it prevents outside influences. I do not consider myself so important that spirits across the block are trying to poke their head into my work. A witch should have familiar spirits who are able to alert the witch to strangers and protect them. There is a certain level of risk involved with raising a crossroads and having something uninvited being drawn but not to the degree where it should be an all-consuming fear. This is why we have the familiar spirit, ancestral spirits, and land spirits on our side long before doing any major works. When you have that kind of backup there's not much that will want to pick a fight with you. This does not include doing cursework because that is its own field and will get its own coverage.

Get chalk and a rag or alternatively cornmeal and a broom. Set up an open space, preferably a designated room, to create the crossroads. Lay out the cornmeal in the shape of an 'X'. Depending on what you are doing you may want to have your target in the center. For instance, if you are attempting to call the Witch Father to manifest you would place a stag or ram skull into the center of the X. This gives a clear indication of what you want and the easiest way to achieve the goal. If you are empowering a talisman, it is placed in the center.

Call your spirits to you. Pull your familiars strength around you, almost like a cloak. Ask the land spirits to keep outsiders where they belong. Bring your ancestors close to you. Tell your spirits why they are there and what you are doing. Make sure they are there to help and won't dip out. Once you have the connection, begin to call the crossroads. Talk to the shape you've made, tell it what it is.

> *"You are the meeting of two roads,*
> *where we dance and sing and cheer for the Witch Father.*
> *Where he comes and drinks with us,*
> *teaches us how the stars move and how the plants grow.*
> *Open your roads so that he may come through."*

Once you feel the sensations you associate with the crossroads (I tend to feel like everything around me has slowed or become unnaturally quiet) then begin addressing the Witch Father to call him to you.

After your work is done, close it down in reverse order. Check your senses, is it still the unnatural calm of the crossroads? Then disrupt the shape a little and address the figure as just cornmeal "You are chicken feed, to be swept up and canned away. There are no guests left here, the sun is coming and we are going." Keep this up until the sensation is past and your spirits have given you the go ahead. Remove any central items and clean up the cornmeal. Some may choose to save it, I tend to throw it away.

If you truly feel something uneasy, throw a banishing powder on the crossroads and sweep it up with a broom. Be careful, because if you do this before the Witch Father is done with the space (and you've mistaken the Witch Father for a strange spirit entering in) you'll probably piss him off.

Thin Places

There are other methods to creating places of power and thin places. Over time ritual actions and phrases will be enough to create the response needed for you to do the work without the rigmarole involved in making a physical crossroads. I typically knock on a wooden surface and recite a Psalm known to my spirits as the signal for making work. I made a specific wooden tablet for just that, wood burned with the Psalm passage on it. This has become its own place of power and replaces the need for a crossroad when doing some works like the creation of a talisman. The tablet is analogous to the Wiccan pentacle in that items that need to be brought to life (charged, in Wiccan terms) are placed on this tablet.

Sitting in doorways is another way to create a thin place without having to really do any work at all. This is because doorways are inherently liminal spaces, so there's no need for a ritual to make it liminal. The backside can be that laying in a doorway can feel silly, and unfortunately when doing making feeling silly is a very common way to undermine what you're doing. Embarrassment is a major killer of magical work. So if you can work in a doorway and overcome any feelings of silliness than do it!

When working outdoors the need to create thin places tends to be less of a focus because there are many areas that are natural thin places. Hills, wells, streams, creeks, woods, any place where trees seem to form a doorway- the list goes on. The most obvious is of course, the crossroads itself. There are plenty of times where manmade structures can act as thin places either due to a particular construction (bridges being between two piece of land) or because of repeated human intervention (a field where a witch frequents becoming a thin place). Because you will lack the protection that is inherent to your home you should always bring a protective talisman on your person when working outdoors if the area is unfamiliar to you. Over time you may choose not to bring it with you, but for first time excursions that layer of protection could make the difference between a pleasant and unpleasant experience.

Time is another factor in liminality, and may be familiar to anyone who has ever heard the phrase "witching hour". The most prominent liminal times are dawn, noon, dusk, and midnight. Dawn and dusk are self-explanatory, while noon and midnight divide days as manmade constructs - all of which can add a little oomph when calling your spirits or leaving the body. There are of course seasonal liminal spaces in those place in which seasons are experienced. Witches living in tropical and subtropical areas (damn you Florida) tend to experience two seasons, a hot wet season and cool dry season.

Chapter Nine

Call of the Familiar

What's a witch without her toad suckling on a hidden witch mark and helping her cross the hedge? The familiar spirit is nearly as complex and varied as the Witch Father. The familiar is a spirit that is in some way bound to the witch through pacts and relationships. The familiar is not the same as a spirit guide or ally found in most contemporary witchcraft practices. The familiar is different due to intimate nature with the witch. Ghosts, toads, fairies, devils, and even angels can take the role of the familiar spirit. They can be initiators in some cases, they can be lovers in others. They could be both.

A pact of some kind is what gives the relationship between witch and familiar its unique power. In folklore the animal familiar suckled from a third nipple of the witch, or drank blood through the witch's mark. That image is what helps remind me of why the familiar is so vastly different from other kinds of spirits a witch may work with. The familiar consumes a bit of the witch, they know the witch in ways no one else can, they take a witch one step closer to the wilds.

The image of the black cat as a witch's familiar is only one version of what the familiar can be to a witch. Many familiars were ghosts that were somehow changed by death to become something more. *The Devil, A Beetle and a Bleeding Toe* gives us some insight to the relationship of the familiar with death. Rindy Sue Gose, who we explore with her relationship to the land in another chapter, receives her familiar three days after being initiated by the Devil. After she became a witch the vilest man in her town died. Rindy took a small medicine bottle, snuck into the funeral, and trapped the man's soul into the body of a beetle. This beetle became her familiar and accompanied her on trips through the keyhole. Rindy would then take the shape of a beetle, or at least became the same size as the beetle, during flight with the soul of the dead man.

This story can suggest a few necromantic elements to becoming a witch but most clearly illustrates a closeness to the dead and power. Rindy share her familiars shape during flight, her familiar drank her blood while she prepared for her flight, and her familiar joined her throughout the flight. I don't think the concept of the witch's sixpence (the death of someone as a direct result of witch initiation) holds truth to it, rather it is that the ghost familiar in this story is a hidden nugget to drive home the diverse relationship witches can have with familiars.

During some initiation rituals an animal is present during the ritual and when the Devil appears he then changes this animal into the witch's familiar. This kind of transformation mirrors what is happening to the witch during initiation, creating a shift into a spiritual creature. For some this could mean that the familiar is both something separate from the witch but still a part of them. For other witches there is no doubt that the familiar spirit is separate.

There is no single ritual for calling or obtaining a familiar, just as there is no single way for a familiar spirit to work with a witch. Traditionally the first meeting with the Devil led to receiving a familiar. It's possible that the reader already has a familiar spirit attending to them, which is yet another reason why I will not be listing any specific ritual that details how to receive a familiar. The witchlore pertaining to familiar spirits is much less descriptive in American folklore and so an observation of familiar spirits in Europe will help give context to what we see in American witchlore.

Emma Wilby's *Cunning Folk and Familiar Spirits* gives a thorough examination of the role of familiar spirits and how they empowered the cunning folk of Early-Modern Europe. Cunning folk are essentially folk magic practitioners who serve their community in a magical capacity. Contemporary uses of the word 'witch' reclaim it as a mostly positive word, despite its original use as something wholly negative throughout the world. Contemporary witches often times are actually looking to fulfill similar roles to cunning folk. Cunning folk were known for their healing work, hex reversal, spirit communication, divination, and love attraction. The movement of traditional witchcraft by and large seeks to bring both the Early-Modern witchcraft and cunning craft into a contemporary lens and practice. Folkloric witchcraft follows that trend but emphasizes the folklore (of any time period) that directly influences the practitioner.

Wilby states that cunning folk in Early-Modern Britain typically had their first interaction with their familiar after experiencing trauma[17]. The familiar typically approached the individual and offered some kind of assistance. The relationship between the two varied from person to person. Some had an almost adversarial relationship, not unlike the way the Devil sometimes beats witches in America. Others had deeply sexual relations with their familiar spirits. Cunning man Andro Man stated that he slept with the Queen of Elphame and had children by her, while the illustrious witch Isobel Gowdie went into great detail about how she slept with the Devil.

What is interesting here is that although almost all records state that witches dealt with "the Devil" there are some tidbits in the confessions that suggest the witches in question thought of the situation very differently. Many times in Scottish witch trials[18] there are phrases like "Witch X slept with the Devil, who she called Y." This suggests that the witches admitted to having a familiar spirit who taught them their craft but did not refer to the spirit as the Devil. Inquisitors though believed that all spirits were demonic in nature and so immediately recorded all of these diverse spirits as The Devil.

The role a familiar plays in magic varies greatly and folklore is not always clear on specifics. The most common role a familiar played for cunning folk is teaching them how to heal the sick[19]. This was sometimes done through direct teaching, giving a specific herb, or by undisclosed transmission of power. The familiar could also provide visions and presumably aid in divination or help the witch fly from the body. For the folkloric witch, the familiar is unlikely to fit into neat categories of purpose.

Contemporary witchcraft is infamous for portraying spirits "of" a given area. One of the major criticism of contemporary witchcraft movements is its treatment of spirits as tools to be used without consideration of the spirit or formation of relationships with spirits. Those who practice traditional and folkloric witchcraft will find that they may have relationships with several spirits, and that they may all overlap in areas of expertise. Coming from a movement that has indoctrinated us into thinking spirits are only as good as their correspondence table, this can be confusing.

As folkloric witches we have to break out of that frame work and start thinking of spirits as diverse and specialized as humans are. You may have a familiar come to you from the Witch Father who assists you in spell craft, spirit flight, and healing while another familiar who comes to you from the land only wants to help you with healing. If the witch in this situation is lucky, or skilled in negotiation, these spirits may have no qualms with working together. However, it is also highly possible that the witch will have to compromise with both spirits in order to ensure they are both able to assist in order to maintain both relationships.

Maintaining relationships with spirits is another foreign concept in contemporary witchcraft. In some forms of contemporary witchcraft spirits are called upon to do a job and then dismissed when the job is done with no second thoughts. Folkloric witches view spirits as having their own autonomy and deserving of compensation for their work. Each familiar will have different likes and dislikes, and is likely to have a certain binding contract with you.

In my personal experience familiars want a regularly scheduled offering and consistent work. It is possible to lose a familiar due to either a lack of payment or not enough work. If we think of this in terms of employment, if we hire someone and don't pay them consummate wages they are likely to leave and find someone who will pay better. If you pay well, but have no work for them to do, they are likely to get bored and seek out someone who will allow them to flourish and increase their own skills.

We have already covered that a witch should keep track of progress and spirit contacts, and this illustrates why this is so important. A large portion of our power comes from our familiars. If we are unable to maintain these relationships, we are unable to maintain our level of skill and working. The more familiar spirits a witch has, the more influence that witch has on the otherworld and the immediate world around themselves. However this also means that the witch must attend to these spirits in a manner that pleases all of them. This can become a very delicate balance and clearly outlines the fact that sometimes quality overrides quantity. To continue our employment metaphor, the more employees you have the more work you can complete and the more revenue you can secure. But this also means getting payrolls straightened out, providing suitable training, and ensuring that no one thinks you are "playing favorites".

Relationship and Role of the Familiar

The Familiar can act as the bridge between ourselves and other spirits who we wish to interact with. The Familiar can be a protector, teacher, helper, ass kicker, and name taker. The Familiar is often thought of as an animal and while animal familiars are numerous in folklore and testimony it is important to note that many familiar spirits were humanlike.

Popular representation of the familiar is that is a servant, which I personally do not agree with. Some testimony actually refers to certain gods as familiar spirits. Looking at the word familiar, there are no connotations of subservience there. There are connotations of family and familiarity. These spirits are close to us, they know us in a way that other spirits simply do not and they can be called upon with a speed that other spirits will not have.

The bond of a familiar spirit is like a marriage in a way, it is a serious binding magical relationship. If you leave each other it can be nasty (and come back to haunt you) or be civil. The spirit may be a very powerful entity, hell some accounts refer to the Devil and a witch's familiar as one and the same. This can also be confusing, as sometimes a witch would talk about a spirit, and clergy would immediately translate that spirit to the Devil so there is some leeway here. The point is, familiars are not your servant.

It is interesting that in many traditions the familiar spirit is literally married to the witch, and that in *The Silver Bullet* there is at least one case where a man marries a spirit/witch. There once was a cat who came to an old man who lived alone. The man had lost his own cat and missed having an animal around. So one night he caught the cat and when he pet it the cat turned into a beautiful woman. The man and woman married and had two children. The man never gave her secret, but one night after too much drinking he let it slip that she was a cat. As soon as he told this she turned back into a cat, along with the children, and left.

This story should exemplify the importance of keeping secrets in your practice. Many folkloric witches keep their practice close to their chest, which has sometimes been misinterpreted as gatekeeping. Writing this book has been an experiment with maintaining secrets while providing examples of how to access the power of folklore. There are certain things that your spirits will not allow you to expose, these things will be pivotal in your practice. The secret will give it power and forces us to fight our natural instinct to share an important part of our lives. Should you go against the wishes of a familiar spirit, expect a consequence including losing that familiar spirit.

Maintaining a Familiar Relationship

Some of y'all are probably visual learners like I am. I may not be able to draw out an example, but by using a hypothetical situation we can start to see what it is like to maintain a relationship with a proper familiar spirit. We will start with one familiar and assume that you have received this familiar from the Witch Father shortly after observing omens for Killing the Moon. The familiar is in the shape of a small mouse, named Dill Tom, and has stated he will assist you in works of divination and repairing relationships for clients. On your first meeting Dill Tom tells you what kind of home he wishes to live in. In order for your familiar to maintain a

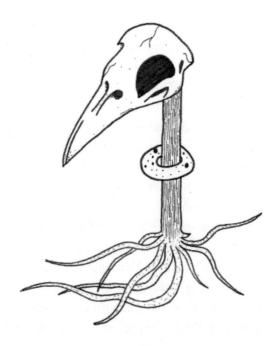

link with you and your work, a spirit house must be constructed. Dill Tom is very particular and wants a circular glass bottle filled with grains and aromatic herbs. Dill Tom also tells you that you will need to burn one of your Tarot cards and place the ashes into the spirit home to link Dill Tom to your divination.

Now you love your tarot cards, in fact you've had them for over five years! You even still have the cardboard box they originally came in! You tell Dill Tom that you cannot do this and ask what compromise can be made. Dill Tom states that since you still have the original box, and the cards have been kept in it when not in use that the ashes of the box will do just as well. You agree that this is a fair compromise and state that the spirit home will be completed within two weeks. Dill Tom gives you a specific time at which to call him. He tells you that this will be the time when he is most able to answer your call thanks to those ingredients and be linked to the spirit home.

Two weeks fly by, and an audit at work has kept you absolutely swamped. During this you realize you have absolutely no aromatic herbs. Did Dill Tom even say if it had to be a certain herb? Is rosemary aromatic enough? It has a strong smell. The time is closing in and you rush to fill the bottle with rosemary. You'd rather be on time with something slightly wrong then late and nothing at all.

You call Dill Tom with some ceremony and flattering praises. You go on about how Dill has the loveliest paws of any rodent you've ever seen! His eyes are more piecing than a hawks! His mind shrewder than a shrew! You feel a prickling on your arms and enter into a light trance state. You are in receptive state and can speak with Dill Tom, who comments on how lovely the bottle smells! You conduct the ritual and link Dill Tom to his new spirit home.

For weeks you navigate Dill's ins-and-outs. You have agreed that offerings will take the form of a daily hello directed towards the spirit bottle in the morning before work, a weekly divination practice session with the bottle on the table nearest you, and a monthly meal of greens and carrots. Over the course of a few months you have begun getting more clients for your tarot reading business and even survived the audit at work.

In this example, you have already run into a lot of upkeep. Your day-to-day life almost prevented the bottle from even being made, and you now have a schedule that includes interactions with this spirit familiar on a daily basis. Imagine doubling this. Two meals a month on separate days (to prevent jealousy) seems manageable. Splitting weekly magical sessions is a little rough but you're making it work and getting better every day! Now try another spirit and three meals a month, three days out of the week you are doing sessions for different skills. You have less time to rest and just relax from work. You start missing sessions with spirit #3, who has left, but you are unable to tell due to being distracted and keep offering three meals monthly. It isn't for another month when Dill Tom reveals through divination that you've been offering food to a spirit who isn't there anymore. It all gets a little confusing and tiring.

Take time between relationships. Just because you see progress doesn't mean it's worth it! Some familiars can even get bitter. Remember that boss you hated and that you told all your friends not to take jobs from? Spirit familiars can be just as bitter! Will it ruin your practice? No of course not, but it may add some unneeded stress.

Creating a Spirit Home

The most common spirit home is a glass bottle, easily purchased at any craft store. These make perfect spirit homes because the contents are easily personalized to each particular spirit and markings can even be added to the outside. Some spirits may have a particular eye way they want the bottle to look. Bottles can be layered by placing the heaviest material on the bottom and carefully stacking everything up until the very top. As children many of us made sand jars with colored sand the same way. Making a spirit bottle is honestly one of the most enjoyable craft projects you can have and allows you to bond with your spirit by creating a functional tool that is ascetically pleasing.

The typical ritual outline can be utilized as with any object that is being enchanted. What differs here is that you do not yet have the working relationship to be able to cloak yourself in the familiar's energy, because the familiar is not there yet! So for this we will follow a slightly modified outline.

Beginning a ritual with some form of cleansing works in two ways. First it sets the headspace for witchcraft, shifting into the mindset of changing the world around you. Second, cleansing removes unwanted spiritual influences that could interfere with the work you are doing. For me personally, the first function is more important because it's far more common for me to need to shift my headspace than it is to kick out some unwanted ghosts.

Next is creating the thin place. The Crossroad Ritual is an example of this, but other options is to have an item that is itself a thin place. I have a wooden tablet, burned with certain psalm phrases and symbols known to my spirits that is a semi-permanent thin place for my spirits to gather with my intent.

Now you will call to your familiars. Use flattery to bring the spirit close to you. This can be off the cuff if you are good at improvising, but if you doubt your sincerity write it down beforehand. If you know the familiar likes something in particular like singing, sing for them! At some point an omen should manifest to let you know that your familiar is there with you. This could be prickling of your scalp, goose flesh, cold chills, or hearing neighborhood dogs barking suddenly.

When your familiar has made their presence known you need to link them to the spirit home. Place your hands on the home and tell it what purpose it serves. "You are a vessel for the spirit Tom Dill. You are his home, his anchor to this world. Through you, his influence on this side is strengthened and magnified. He will roost here and leave you to create change. You will protect him and remain a tether for him here." Baptize the house in water, oil, or blood. Blood is a much more preferred substance to tether a familiar into place.

Finally you'll close down the ritual by leaving your spirits offerings as payment for work rendered and possibly using ritual gestures to let everyone know that you're done. Some ritual gestures that are common among witches I know would be clapping your hands four times, flipping over a ritual item, or placing a cloth over a working table. As long as you communicate to your spirits what the action means, what that action looks like doesn't make a huge difference. After closing the ritual you may choose to leave the spirit home to rest inside a black bag or cloth. I had an old friend in the Wiccan community tell me that they would do this so that the tool has time to situate itself in its new home, and she liked the idea that it mirrored how newborns are put in a nursery after birth.

In addition to a bottle, other objects may be used as a spirit home. Skulls and statues related to the spirit in some way are very visceral ways to house your familiar. When using a skull it has become a common practice to "redden" the bones during the ritual process by rubbing red ochre on the skull to mimic the blood and muscle of the animal while calling to it. Those who work with spirits traditionally opposed to iron may want to refrain from this particular practice due to the presence of iron in red ochre pigments. Some practitioners may find it suitable to use a drop of their own blood as a link and binding force for the familiar.

Chapter Ten

Ghosts in the Land – Meeting Nature Spirits in the South

Various animistic cultures throughout the world have names for land spirits and very specific descriptions of what these spirits are. America has become a country of immigrants, meaning that the names and descriptions of land spirits from across the world have come here. Given the diversity of American people, the spirits of the land are not easy to pin down. There are no traditional land spirits of the American South and because of this my discussion here is largely from a contemporary witchcraft and unverified personal gnosis (UPG) point of view.

It is important to discuss that colonization is inherently involved in this topic for the United States. Indigenous People have always been incredibly diverse with their own traditions, and I would venture to say that concepts of land spirits (if present in a given tribe) did not always line up. So when talking about America as a whole, I stand by the statement that there is no singular traditional land spirit. Not to mention that as witches we are not privy to the Indigenous traditions (unless raised within them) and so my perspective on this subject comes from a legacy of European colonization and immigration. It is not that I wish to ignore Indigenous traditions, but rather it is neither my place nor my right to discuss those traditions.

Although there are no "traditional land spirits" in the US there are a multitude of spirits that are tied to places and landscapes. Many of these pop up in urban legends as ghosts, devils, or even cryptids. Urban legends contain valuable bits of information that lend itself to the creation of a personal relationship with spirits of the land. In addition to urban legends there are certain ancestors of place that can sometimes fulfill the area of Land

77

Spirits. This is also where things can sometimes be difficult to navigate if you are a European descendant living on unseated Indigenous land, battle grounds, or slave plantations. Further, there are numerous contemporary witchcraft views of land spirits that take an animistic perspective to view how a witch interacts with the land.

There are so many cultures that intersect and cross in the States that it would be impossible to cover each unique land spirit from each tradition. Instead I encourage the reader who is drawn to a particular cultural view of land spirits to seek out apprenticeship or material written by someone who belongs to that culture.

Haunted Land - Urban Legends

Urban legends are the living legacy of oral storytelling. Most modern story telling comes through the creative lens of television, digital media, or music. The art of traditional word of mouth storytelling, of scary stories around the campfire, seems to have taken a backseat in our culture. Scary stories still give us insight to basic ideas of the land and our relationship to the land.

I spent my childhood divided between suburban Maryland, suburban Pennsylvania, and rural Florida. The story telling and urban legends of these places demonstrated to me how landscapes shape communities and identity. In Maryland camping is much more common, the temperate weather allows for a lot of nature excursions that aren't as easy to manage in the Florida heat. Camping meant total disconnect from technology, meaning my treasured GameBoy and Pokémon were left at home. My entertainment came from the stories adults and older kids would tell. I remember hearing about the Maryland Goat Man for the first time camping on Kent Island in Chesapeake Bay.

The goat man story has many variations - sometimes demonic and sometimes science gone wrong. The story as told to me was that a woman with a particularly nasty disposition had given birth to her only son, and her nastiness made the baby deformed. The goat man was the physical manifestation of negative emotions. He was jealous of young boys who got to live normal lives. He stalked families going away on camping trips and would kill the youngest son and try to replace the son, hoping that the family wouldn't notice the difference. At this point in the story telling an older adult, hiding in the bushes, would come screaming out of the woods holding an axe and scarring us kids for life.

This variation was obviously heavily tailored by my family to make it particularly scary for us, and was something I spread at other camping trips when I became older. It became a rite of passage, to spend the night in fear of the goat man- and survive. At the time we didn't look at it that way, mostly it was just the fun of pranking someone else. But as an adult and a witch, I can look at these stories through a different lens. The Goat Man becomes a spirit of fear, healthy fear of the woods and the dangers of the wild. The Goat Man is an example of how scary stories can influence magical practice by shaping how a witch views the spirits roaming the land. This story was much more influential than most stories I heard growing up, especially when compared to the stories in other states I grew up in.

For several years I lived in a small Pennsylvania town full of ghosts. This small town was known for having long, narrow, and winding roads. As kids we would occasionally hear about haunted roads, but as teenagers we could actually go hunt the ghosts ourselves. One friend had heard of a faceless ghost who could be found roadside on the way out of town. We piled into an old beater and went ghost hunting for NoFaceBitch. We were sixteen. None of us where writing best sellers, it was the best name we could come up with.

We had a blast reminiscing, talking about other ghost stories, but after about thirty minutes of no NoFace we had given up and were ready to go home. Then the radio cut out. I tried adjusting it and fixing it, but we figured we had just lost connection from the tree coverage. Then we saw her. Long black hair flowing over pale shoulders and a glowing, featureless face. Something cold, clammy, and terrifying deep inside of me started to stir. We screamed and sped off. After another ten minutes of "what the fuck was that" we realized we had to turn around. We finally did when the radio cut back on.

All of us had our eyes in a different direction, committed to having every corner monitored so she couldn't sneak up on us. As we rounded the corner we saw a figure. A tall man, wearing all white, a black shirt hung around his neck. We all noticed that he was so pale, when the headlights hit his face it made it impossible to see any detail on his face. We had found NoFace, and he was a drunk.

Where I grew up in Florida very few of the urban legends surrounded the supernatural. At least none of the stories that my family told. When my family moved back to Florida they became much more deeply religious and stories of the supernatural became inappropriate. There were some gator-men stories and skunk apes, but nothing that I had much interest in at the time. I have to admit, I grew up terrified that gator-men would break into my house and eat me thanks to my cousins stories. I

think these few stories I had in Florida helped shape my view of nature as a dangerous place, they warned me that I was no longer safe roaming the forests or swimming local creeks like I was in Maryland.

Legends tell us about the world we live in. When exploring the world of land spirits, it may be of use to explore these legends further the same way we have been exploring folklore. The premise of this practice is that we don't have to look far to find meaningful spiritual direction in our lives. We can look to our backyards. Myth, urban legend, and folklore can be examined on the same level when talking about how it impacts our culture, community, and identity. We certainly don't have to use these stories. I know I won't be leaving out offerings to NoFaceBitch anytime soon, but the process of seeking the stories can lead to something meaningful.

Some witches have found that their local land spirit is the very urban legends that surround them. One of my major influences in exploring the tales I grew up with was the work of Tara Maguire and Chris Orapello of the *Down at the Crossroads* Podcast[20]. By looking towards folklore they built a localized tradition that heavily incorporated the Jersey Devil as a central land spirit. I find this concept heavily inspiring, and in their podcast Orapello and Maguire discuss that the techniques are applicable to anyone, but the spirits are local.

This concept is important as it is one of the ways in which folkloric witchcraft differs from other forms of contemporary witchcraft. We are not attempting to call of spirits from halfway across the world, we are looking at the here and now to embrace the land we currently live on rather than the land our ancestors lived on. While calling ancestral deities is also valid, it is not the work of this book.

I have spent extensive amounts of time combing through the local lore of where I currently live. Growing up I was not exposed to the supernatural side of Florida, and that has been a road block for some years. However by digging a little deeper into recorded stories I found tales about some local landmarks that are steeped in magic and have given validity to some of my long held personal beliefs about the land. This includes stories about great towers said to be the home to fairy folk, swamp witches who take the form of owls, and even Florida itself being a suburb of hell.

Depending on where we live we may have stories that have

strong supernatural ties, superficial teenage tales, or just a fantasized version of the reality of where we live. So while this approach can be empowering, it is not the only way to explore working with the land.

Ancestors of the Land - Navigating a History of Violence

The history of the United States is not a pretty one. In most cases where we live is unseated indigenous land that was taken by blood, coercion, and force. Those of us living in the South live on a legacy of slavery and racism that cannot and should not be swept under the rug. We live in places that celebrate slavery and continue these legacies of racism today. The hero worship of Robert E. Lee is incredibly prevalent in the South and is often passed off as remembering history or celebrating Southern pride. This is despite the fact that Lee was a traitor to the country and many places that erect statues of him did so not after the Civil War, but in the 1960's as a reaction to growing anti-racist and civil rights movements.

The dead of these lands continue to exist today, and are not blind to what is happening. In my experience I have found that some of these dead have become integrated into the land as protectors. I refer to these spirits as Ancestors of Place or Ancestors of the Land. As a white Southerner there have been many uncomfortable moments with reconciling the realty of American history and working with spirits of the land. I encourage all witches to embrace these uncomfortable realities and do extensive research on the land they live on.

We exist solely because of the actions of our ancestors. We are born and thrive due to what our ancestors did before us. Some of these ancestors may have had no choice in where they ended up because of the atrocity of the slave trade, sharecropping, Jim Crow, or the genocide of Native Americans. Some of our ancestors may have tried to stop it, while some have actively contributed to these atrocities. If we expect to have a relationship with the land, we have to come to terms with the past and present oppression of the peoples who have lived on this land.

I continue to state that this path is one where every witch will have unique experiences, but when it comes to ancestor work, including ancestors of place, unique is an understatement. If you are a person of color living on what used to be a plantation you may have a very different experience with those spirits than a white person would. Take mind, I'm not saying negative, just different. This work is inherently emotional, problematic, and difficult. There are many aspects of who you are and what the land has experienced that could cause unique challenges.

Often I make contact with the Ancestors of the Land to thank them for giving me space to safely live on, I give them offerings, and that is kind of the end of it. Over time if the spirits and I have grown to trust each other I may ask for protection while doing a working or during natural disasters. So although land spirits are incredibly important in my craft, it isn't because they help me with my craft but rather because I would not be here without their approval. Locations that do have Ancestors of Place pose interesting challenges and learning experiences for witches.

The Land Itself - American Animist

Something very important to remember when you are trying to form relationships with the land is that the land may not want to form relationships with you. In fact, the land might want to kill you. This is not an idea that jives well with most modern pagans who grew up in the "Light and Love" era but it's important to talk about nonetheless. Humans have a long history of abusing the land. You are a human. No matter how magical and earth loving, you are a human. You contribute to pollution in many ways, even though you may actively be trying to be as environmentally conscious as possible. I know I'm guilty of this, because I drive my car everywhere due to a lack of public transportation and large distances that make it almost impossible to effectively bike or walk. That being said I have still formed deep and meaningful bonds with many spirits in my area, however I know of several places where the spirits trust no one and I keep my distance when possible.

The spirits who don't want to work with you as a witch should not discourage you in any way! We live how we can and unfortunately not everyone can be as green as they would like to be. There are still spirits that will gladly work with you, and just because a spirit doesn't want to work with you right now doesn't mean it won't work with you at a later point in time. Some spirits may actually tell you everything you need to create a relationship with the land. We've already looked at two unique kinds of spirits that may be included as local spirits in your area, both of which are things to be conscious of as American witches. Now we look at spirits that can be thought of as the literal embodiment of the land itself. These are spirits that are tied very specifically to the geographic location or where you are and hold little to no sway outside of its bounds. Meaning these are the literal spirits of place including house spirits, the spirit of a city, or the spirit of a county.

As an animist I see all things as being imbued with spirit. The local creek, the buildings around me, even small stones are uniquely their own. These spirits interact in ways that are unique to any other kind of spirits, which will be discussed at length when talking about plant spirits. Beginning a relationship with your land is, normally, very simple. Depending on the extent of how the spirit is involved in your craft, maintaining the relationship can range from casual friendship to deep familiar bond. I will detail methods of how to work with spirits in a few different living situations, but of course I will not be able to cover everything.

I cannot stress enough how unique this aspect of witchcraft is, because every place in the United States is so unique. I have lived on the edges of small swamps, in major cities, in historic coastal towns, and in the middle of nowhere and each time bonding with the spirits has been completely different. You will find that starting from scratch every time you move is incredibly bittersweet and can differ greatly from the experiences of others. There are many new age streams of witchcraft that circumvent this by worshiping a Mother Goddess figure who can be a sort of middle woman between a worshiper and the land spirits. This is a valid approach in its own rights, but will not be detailed here as it involves religious aspects that are not a part of this practice.

Embodied Spirits

Embodied spirits are spirits who are personifications of the land itself. Unlike other spirits such as Gods or familiars, these spirits cannot be invoked outside of their domain. They are the literal land, and as such cannot move in ways that other spirits can. There are some ways around this however, such as carrying a bit of soil or dirt from your home when you go on a trip acts as a talisman to return you home safely. By and large however working with these spirits is done on the land where they are.

Land spirits can sometimes appear in a spectral or anthropomorphic shape in visions, often times that is simply easier for us as humans to conceive of spirits. Sometimes they may take the shape of local fauna and flora. Where I live the local embodied spirit often appears in the shape of a gator. In more wild areas such as swamps or forests, the spirits may literally appear to you as a flesh and blood animal or by moving plants. In my experience land spirits work their magic best through experience rather than visions.

A land spirits behavior will be strongly shaped by the kind of people who have lived or traveled through there in the past. Land spirits that have been tended by the same family for generations may not take kindly to a strange family moving in and may cause problems in the home. From what I've seen land spirits are the second biggest cause for spiritual mischief in the home, behind ancestors. However as long as you are respectful, acknowledge the land spirits, and acknowledge that this land is theirs and not yours- you should have few problems.

Land Spirits of large areas like counties or states may have a central feature that can be thought of as its home. This can be very wild areas (such as the Florida Everglades) or particular trees that have stood the test of time. One such tree in Florida was The Senator, a tree that most locals said was around 3,500 years old. An arsonist burned the tree down in 2012, and the pain felt throughout the state was a testament to how deeply the spirit of this tree (literally and figuratively) effected the state's residents. These locations could provide pilgrimage sites for you to deepen that relationship, and could also act as a way to show your local spirits the respect you have for them. Again this is very subjective, and you may find that state wide land spirits don't resonate with you- that's fine. Even on your local land you should be able to identify somewhere that acts as a focal point for land spirits.

Roles of Land Spirits in Witchcraft

Your local spirits will tell you exactly what they can be called on for, so this list will be short. I know some folks who petition their city spirits for clear traffic, good rental deals, and even meeting a good romantic partner so don't let this list shorten your expectations by any means. While it is helpful to keep in mind the ways that Land Spirits can help us in our craft, that is not why we work with them. Land Spirit work is about maintaining a balance with things much older than us, not what they can do for us.

Land spirits often first engage with me as protective spirits during a working. They are addressed first in the working and are asked to watch over the participants and to deter outsiders from interrupting. This includes outsiders who are physical and may disrespect the participants, as well as spirits who are not welcome.

Some land spirits will gladly share their power or expertise with you while working. These spirits who bring empowerment may become mentors, familiars, or even initiators under certain circumstances.

One of the more practical sides of working with land spirits is getting their assistance with growing and maintaining plants. Growing something with your own two hands is an experience that any witch should at least try. I have a small garden on my patio of about 15-20 different species at any time. The spirits I work with are city spirits, so these plants keep me in touch with the land in ways I would not be able to otherwise. The land spirits are very protective of my garden and there are many times I have asked for their help in fending off insects or large invasive lizards.

Basic Introductions

Regardless of the kind of environment you live in, all land spirits interactions will start in essentially the same way. You introduce yourself, tell the land why you are there (maybe butter up the spirits by telling them how wonderful they are) and leave some kind of simple offering. My favorite is an apple which I normally leave somewhere significant on the landscape. In regards to offerings, be aware of how you may inadvertently damage the locality by leaving certain offerings. Avoid leaving fruits with seeds that may propagate an invasive plant in that area and potentially harm the land. Leaving fully cooked meals may be harmful to the animals who are likely to eat up whatever you leave. It may also be pertinent to research taboos held on the land. For instance folks in the American Celtic Reconstructionist community tend to avoid pouring alcohol directly onto the earth as some First Nations people believe that this is a harmful practice. Out of respect for those living cultures whose land rights have been infringed upon many CR's choose alternative ways to offer their spirits alcohol that does not include pouring it directly onto the earth.

Throughout your time on the land you will want to simply address the spirits and talk for a bit. It is important to build a relationship by offering up your time more than just food or drink. Just don't expect a spirit to fall in love with you after one offering. It's time, not things, which really build trust. When it comes to land spirits that trust is incredibly important for all the injustice that humans have dealt to the land.

Take time to know the spirits before asking for any involvement in your practice. Life is transient, and witchcraft is very personal. There's no need to ask a spirit to become deeply ingrained in your practice if you plan on moving within the next year or two. So be comfortable with taking time to know a spirit. After establishing a relationship I like to ask the spirits if they would be interested in being involved in my craft. I would say there's normally a 50/50 split. Land Spirits who are the embodiment of the land itself tend to enjoy being involved in many aspects of my craft. Ancestors of the land normally prefer to play a kind of protective role, if any at all. When I lived in St. Augustine Florida I found that the ancestors of place there (a diverse mix of Spanish Catholic, French Huguenot, and Timicuan Natives) enjoyed the relationships building but did not want to be involved in witchcraft. So by use of divination or spirit communication see what the spirits are comfortable with and respect those boundaries.

Once I have established that relationship and those boundaries I normally include the spirits on my altar in some way. I have used a gator paw to represent and tie to the spirits of the swamp which surround me for over five years. Bones and animal parts, leaves, twigs, branches, stones, even water can all be powerful ties to the land and should be very locally sourced. While working outdoors the land spirits are the first addressed as I am in their domain. While indoors, I honor them but have a stronger focus on house spirits and personal familiars. I consider house spirits to be a part of the family of land spirits, and take similar approaches when working with them.

Largely the discussion surrounding land spirits is centered on the land on which the witch lives on. However many times places we visit may have much more active spirits than where we live. In my experience, addressing land spirits of swamps and forests often times provoke something much more powerful than the land I live on. Going in to wild places to address spirits has given me real, no-shit moments of spirit influence in my life. So while there is an idealized version of how things should work, at the end of the day we can't hold ourselves back because of the expectations we've read about.

Beyond Friendship - The Witch's Tree

Multiple times in the witch lore we see a tree as the center of a witch's power. The tree seems to act as a familiar, as an oath, as a power source. The tree may be the meeting place for the Devil, but in some cases it appears to me that the tree actually replaces the role of devil-initiator. In an animistic world view, this is completely valid. Those who own land may look to the ritual below in order to establish a permanent relationship with their land spirits in a way that will tie yourself and your descendants to the land.

Those who do not own land may still experience this kind of initiation-by-land but the effects may be different. To be initiated by the spirits of the land does not mean that you are forever bound to the land physically. Initiation by land can however create a longing in your heart for the land that taught you its secrets. The initiation into its secrets are not the spiritual death of the other rituals listed, but no matter where you go you will always miss the essence of that place. You may long to run besides the deer in your hometowns forest, ache for the low rumble of a gator wading through a swamp, or be haunted by the sounds of waves across the shore. Of course this experience of land-sickness isn't just for witches, anyone who has left land they love experience this. So how you experience this relationship will be determined by the length of time you spend on the land, what the land means to you, and the way in which you form a bond with the spirits of the land.

By looking at folklore we can get a glimpse of how a witch tree works and the forms the spirits of the land may take. The story *The Devil, a Beetle and a Bleeding Toe*[21] tells us about the witch Rindy Sue Gose and her witch tree. She approaches a particular birch tree and draws a ring around the tree. She draws a cross in the ring then "whispers some mumble jumble sich as we'd never heard afore" and begins to dance. Rindy dances like this for 13 nights in a row and on the 13th night she brings a black hen to the tree and sacrifices it. She pours the blood on the tree and throws the body of the hen into the woods. Where the hen falls, the Devil appears and initiates Rindy by having her sign her name in the book and giving her a witch mark. The two danced and parted ways.

Later in the book there is a story called *The Strange Chestnut Tree* which provides us with more information on what a witch's tree looks like. The witch in this story eats the chestnuts to shape shift into various animals and has to keep the tree safe or lose his power. A local man tries to chop down the tree and is struck dead by a witchball.

In *The Granny Curse* there is a story about a young deer who is shot with a peach pit by a hunter who lost his bullets. This deer survived, but instead of growing stag horns, it grew a peach tree straight out of its head. The peaches grew all years, and the hunter's wife could call the deer to her so she could make the best damn peach pies you've ever had.

These stories show us some very different ideas about magical trees and their roles among land spirits. The Devil in Rindy's story may very well be the spirit of the birch tree itself rather than the enemy of Christ. The chestnut tree becomes a source of shapeshifting, which is intimately tied to contemporary spirit flight techniques. And the deer with a peach tree is the most land spirit creature I've ever heard of. So there are plenty of benefits to working with a Witch's Tree.

Ritual of the Witch Tree

You must know the land intimately. You must know the names of the animals, plants, streams, and spirits that cross through your land. You must find a tree that stands apart, an anchor to the local spirits, a beacon of this land. Go to the tree and tell it why you've come. Draw a ring around the tree, signal to it that you are here to dance for it. For thirteen nights dance with the tree and return home. On the final night give the tree a taste of your blood, a sign of respect and an offering of power. Mark a crossroads into the dirt and ask the spirit to use your blood to appear before you. When the tree's spirit has been palpably conjured make a pact with the spirit. Dance with your ally and return to your home.

Return regularly to dance with the tree, to learn from it and to be given its power. Take the fruit and the flowers to perform your craft. Be careful about when and how you take because to damage the tree is to damage yourself and your relationship with the land.

The Witch's Broom

Along with the cauldron this is kind of the quintessential witch related tool. While most traditional witches that I have met use the broom as a tool for spirit flight, this has never really drawn me in. After the time I've spent combing through Southern folklore I've found that it wasn't all that common of a motif there. For years I always thought brooms were pretty, but never felt moved to make one. I met witches who would dish out hundreds of dollars on fine crafted ash and birch brooms for rituals, and while that's dandy it just ain't for me. I make a living, but not enough to afford fabulous ritual tools that I may never use.

It wasn't until I stumbled upon an old Southern craft book that I became obsessed with the idea of making my own broom. I was taking a trip to my birth town for the first time in about 10 years. My partner and I were rifling through a local antique shop when I picked up *By Southern Hands* by Jan Arrow and turned to a random page only to stumble upon an old Florida craft: the palmetto broom. For those who don't know, Palmetto's are like a palm trees angry ole' granny. Sharp as an axe and so low to the ground they sneak up on ya' and rip straight through your clothes and skin. I've been scratched by more of these buggers than I can even count. The idea of making brooms out of them seemed perfect. I didn't have the money to buy the book and without any kind of instructions I wasn't sure where to go next.

I figured, what the hell I'll just go cut some palmettos and palms and figure it out. I cut off five palm branches from right outside my door, grabbed some twine and a pocket knife then went to work. I bundled the branches together, got my partner to hold them in place, and wrapped the twine around some key points to keep everything from moving. My partner and I sang some songs, told jokes, and finished in under an hour. During this process I ended up cutting my finger and getting blood onto the palm. That kind of changed the experience for me. I started this to get closer to a local and frugal craft, but when my blood hit that palm I felt different about it.

I felt as though this process brought me closer to my land in a new way, and incorporated my land into my practice for the first time. Sure I'd given offerings and talked to spirits plenty, but this was the first time I made something of the land that truly was becoming a part of my practice. We finished and I sealed off the twine with a little wax to keep it all together.

It was a little messy, a little jagged, but it was mine. When I held it, I felt like I could beat back any nasty bugger that could come my way. I didn't do much by the way of ceremony to make it a craft tool, I didn't need to. It had already tasted my blood, it was already a part of my craft. I didn't need ash and birch, didn't need a blackthorn staff or any such foreign wood. Just palm, which I had never had any fond feelings for. Now I love the thing, and seeing the trees I once thought of as a tourist trap makes me feel like I'm looking at a neighbor of mine.

The Witch's Broom should be made from local materials. Wood is nice because it lasts longer, but mine is made strictly of palm fronds and it works just fine. The broom acts as a direct connection to the land for me, and a stiff protector. Its job is to clear. I sweep before laying the crossroad to clear up the space for liminal work, and I sweep up the cornmeal after to clear away what's left of the crossroads. No real ritual here, just whatever's in your gut.

Personal Experience with the Spirits of the Land

My partner and I love hiking. Here in Southwest Florida where everything is flat, it's more just walking aimlessly in a vaguely wooded area. Every time we go out I make a point to leave an apple for the spirits of the land. On one such occasion we were walking through a pine woodland a few towns over, and I found a small mound that was flanked by two tall, limbless trees. To me this marked an obvious sacred place, where you enter a portal made of trees to climb this very slight incline. I introduced myself, stated my business, walked between the trees and left an apple at the top of the mound. Then we went about our trip and spent a good three hours just walking in the cool December air (which in Florida is still about 70°F).

We found a place where the trail split into three paths and decided to lay down for a bit. This area was unique in that there were no ant hills, plenty of shade, and very little signs of other biting insects that normally cover every surface imaginable. We had a moment of peace, where it seemed as if everything outside of this forest no longer existed. It was profound, not in grand visions or out of body experience, but just peaceful in a moment where I was at least nominally safe for the very real dangers present in any wild area.

When we got up we realized that we had no clue which way we had come from, or where the best exit was. This wasn't a national park, just a local fishing and walking trail, so we had no signs or maps to tell us where to go. We weren't too concerned, knowing that eventually we would be able to walk out of there, but we also didn't want to end up on the opposite side of where we had parked.

So I closed my eyes, took a deep breath and asked for help from the spirits of the land. I stated who I was, and where I had left my offering. I then asked for assistance getting to our car. Before I could finish my sentence, a plant with long leaves protruding from the ground started moving. There was no breeze, no animals or insects brushing against the plant. It almost looked like it was dancing. I said hello and asked if the plant could help guide us out. The plant stopped bouncing, but another plant about 20 feet ahead of us started bouncing. This went on like this, plants starting and stopping bouncing at about 20-30 feet intervals until we found the exit. At the end I expressed my gratitude to the spirits of the forest and left another apple at the last bouncing plant.

When we were completely out of the forest we noticed that we were only about a five minuet walk to our car. My partner grabbed my arm and said "What was that" in an obvious state of disbelief. I shrugged my shoulder and said "I guess we have new friends."

Chapter Eleven

Hi Ho! Through the Keyhole I Go!

There are women who hide their skin in a trunk. They cover themselves in grease and don red caps to fly through the air. They steal milk and ride men like horses till they collapse from exhaustion. They slip through keyholes, and go to other worlds.

Witches in the South don't have stangs or brooms so much as some grease and a hat to fly in. Spirit flight is ubiquitous with traditional witchcraft and the absolute most sought after skill in a witch's bag of tricks. Spirit flight is also the practice most filled with expectations and a desire to master overnight. It is quite possibly one of the most difficult things to achieve on your own in the practice of witchcraft.

Witches in folklore often have grease that they slathered on and slipped out of their skin with. This grease let them literally fold up their skin and fly through keyholes or chimneys. Witch grease is synonymous with the topical flying ointments of European witchcraft, composed of poisonous plants rendered into animal fat to help the witch enter trance and leave their body. Flying ointments in Europe were said to take a witch's spirit out of the body to the Sabbath, underworld, or even the realms of fairy[22.]

In folklore witches fly in order to steal from others, to hag ride enemies, and to go drinking with the Devil. For witches today flying is all of those things, but it is largely about meeting with the spirits on their own turf. Flying can be done to learn from spirits, to make pacts on their side of the fence, or to take something from the other side and bring it back to our side. Flying is an ecstatic approach to leaving the body. Flying is not easy and it takes a long time to build up a practice. Contemporary witches who are familiar with the practice of astral projection will be familiar with the amount of work that goes into leaving the body.

Flying is done in many ways and is characterized differently by every practitioner I've spoken to. Phrases that have similar meanings in other magical circles include astral projection and crossing the hedge. Flying is distinguished by its ecstatic aspects which can include using entheogens, fasting, and dancing until they receive visions and out of body experiences.

Flight

Creating and maintaining a practice of spirit flight is one of the more difficult aspect of witchcraft because it brings to light a lot of doubt that many of us have at some point in regards to spirit work. Full flight is the leaving of the body in ecstasy, it is dangerous and exhilarating, and often times out of our control. Most contemporary witches come to this practice from a meditative standpoint, which is valid and incredibly useful for easing into leaving the body. Many witches expect to have overnight success and really push the envelope to leave the body, and when they cannot immediately dance at the Sabbath they begin to question the legitimacy of their practice.

Struggling to achieve spirit flight is very common and shouldn't make you question the authenticity of your craft. If you ease yourself into the practice and stay with it you will see results. There are some techniques we find through history and anthropology that can shed some light on how to improve the methods used for spirit flight. In the book *Cunning Folk and Familiar Spirits* author Emma Wilby presents the hypothesis that narratives of cunning folk and witches meeting with familiar spirits are indicative of visionary experiences not unlike those experienced by traditional shamanic practitioners. She presents evidence from several sources, most notably from confession narratives given by British cunning folk.

The term visionary experience in the context of Wilby's book refers to seeing spirits but I find that the details could also be useful for out of body experiences like spirit flight. Some of the key elements during visions as stated in confessions are spontaneity of the experience[23], deep emotional states, food and sleep deprivation, and pushing the body past its limit[24]. During a state in which an individual experienced these excruciating circumstances they were more likely to have visions of spirits.

These circumstances were a part of daily life, and not an attempt by the individual to seek out the spirits. In fact, most historical sources emphasize the desire of most folks to stay as far away from spirits and faeries as possible. As witches we engage in atypical relationships with spirits and embrace the more wild nature of these spirits. So while these cunning folk may have stumbled upon their spiritual relationships, witches can seek out relationships by looking at these conditions through a different lens.

Of course this must be done carefully and with full accountability of how fasting, sleep deprivation, and self-exertion can effect physical and mental health. Taking into account personal health and social needs a witch can alter their daily routine in ways that can set them up for success.

Precautions

Before any attempt to use an entheogen you should become very familiar with the substance. Flying ointments are known to contain poisons, and even flying ointments that don't contain poisons may still cause allergic reactions. Plants are not always safe and it's important to be well informed on the possible side effects of using unfamiliar plant material in any aspect of your witchcraft. Incense blends, flying ointments, and tinctures can all cause side effects and can all interact with existing medication. Before using any plants magically you should research its effects on the body or speak to a doctor.

Choosing a specific day to attempt spirit flight is important.

We have jobs, families, and responsibilities to consider. Spirit flight is exhausting and can create a kind of hang-over effect for some people. So find a day that you can reasonably set aside strictly for magical work.

Once you have picked a day you'll want to tailor your diet for the day. I normally restrict the times when I eat, without risking putting my body into shock of course. Do this with some knowledge of your body and what kind of fasting would be appropriate for your health. For me this means fruits and vegetables, limited caffeine, no meats and no sugary snacks. Some folks I know fast from sun up till sun down to great effect but I know my body well enough to know that won't sit well.

Breaking up your sleep pattern will also aide in vision seeking. This is done the night before the flight and essentially includes setting alarms at regular intervals to break your sleep and get yourself into a liminal state.

Finally you come to the actual attempt by using ritual tools and dance. You'll want to perform this in a liminal state so either by finding a thin place outside or by creating a crossroads inside. The importance of protective spirits is imperative to spirit flight. If you do not have at least three spirits that can accompany you I wouldn't even worry about attempting spirit flight yet. These spirits do not necessarily have to be familiars. They could be land spirits, ancestors, the Witch Father, etc. One spirit should be protecting your physical body, another should be flying with you in spirit, and a third should be around just in case something goes wrong. I would also suggest having a friend or partner be with you to ensure that you can come back to your body with no interference.

Once protections and precautions are taken care of apply a little test patch of your grease to make sure you won't have any adverse effects. Wait about 20-30 minutes to make sure you feel okay and nothing strange is happening. Then apply your grease to your armpits, back, or feet[25] about 30-40 minutes before you intend to dance. If you are dancing outside feel free to lather up your feet, but if you are dancing inside on hardwood or linoleum you may want to reconsider the danger of busting your ass. Put on any specially made clothes and begin dancing once you feel the effects of the grease. Scope out the area before hand for any ant hills, rocks, or dangerous debris. Nothing will shock you back to your body more than fire ants taking a bite out of ya'.

Dance until you are exhausted, calling on your spirits and spiritually removing your skin. Dance until you absolutely cannot anymore and when you fall immediately send your body out into the world. Don't allow yourself to get caught up in self-doubt even for a second, just send your body out.

When you return from the flight make sure that you have some water and food, treat yourself. Flying is hard work and you've deserved it. Close down the way you would any ritual, taking extra care to check yourself and your space for any changes or anything attempting to follow you back. Like most rituals, details are excluded for you to tailor to your needs. There are some ritual tools and talismans that can be particularly powerful for a Southern witch to use in flight and vision seeking.

Making the Witch's Grease

Witch's Grease or Flying Ointment is going to be your best friend for spirit flight. You can purchase ointment online from a reputable witch or make it yourself. I have done both and found the process to be much more deeply empowering to create your own ointment. There can sometimes be a lot of trial and error, and a lot of research on poisons, but very powerful experiences overall.

An ointment is not just a tool or something to be used, it is a powerful spirit in its own right. If you are planning on making your own ointment it should be done by acknowledging the autonomy of each plant and bringing them together to create a unique spirit. This is more manageable if you are growing the plants yourself because you become intimately familiar with their needs and potency.

As I am not a trained herbalist I make absolutely no suggestions or recommendations as to what a Witch's Grease should have specifically in it. The folklore in America is equally vague and only occasionally hints at its origin by calling it "lard" (meaning an animal fat base) or stating that some witches use two different kinds of grease one to take her skin off and one to help her fly[26]. I take this as being a shove towards learning more about local plant life to create a flying ointment. There are of course some staples in European witchlore that include mandrake, belladonna, datura, henbane, and wormwood. These poisons are what make it a flying ointment as opposed to an herbal ointment. It is the poisons that, when applied topically and never internally, create the liminal trance state which make flight accessible.

I made my flying ointments from plants that I grew myself and that thrived in my environment, including a poisonous plant that I took time to learn from before cultivating. I lived in my locale for three years before doing this and I would suggest that a witch take a good amount of time knowing the local plants before doing the same. Most ointments are a base of oils and animal fats, however I have made mine from wax rather than fats.

The actual process of creating the ointment starts with growing the plants or locating them for wildcrafting. A relationship should be established with the spirits of the plants, research should be done on the active compounds in the plants, and interactions that may take place between active ingredients should be well researched as well. Just because two plants are in the same family doesn't mean they won't combine to have incredibly adverse side effects. When the time to harvest has come leave an equivalent offering. You'll want to hang the plants to dry. This could take days to a few weeks depending on the plant and part.

A word of caution when drying out herbs and plants, be incredibly mindful of mold. I grow a specific kind of flowering plant that comes in a variety of species. I had been using one variety for a few years in my flying ointments and never had a single issue drying it out. Last year I received a variation that grew double-trumpeted flowers, meaning that one flower grew inside of another. I tried drying these the same way I always had, not taking into account that the interior flower would be drying at a different rate entirely. When it came time to harvest them, I lost over twelve flowers to mold because I didn't take into account how the plant differed from my original plant.

Once your plants have dried, set aside tools specifically for using poisonous herbs. A knife, cutting board, funnel, filter, and double boiler will be needed. I cannot stress enough that these should not be used for any kind of cooking once used for this purpose. Chop the plant material into smaller bits and put them into a specially prepared canning jar. You'll cover the plant material in oil and let it for a bit sit. You could do a cold infusion, letting the oil extract the active compounds over several weeks in a cool dark place in which case put aside until it's time to continue on. If you are doing a hot infusion you will place the jar in the double boiler and allow it to heat up slowly over time. This process typically takes about two hours, keeping a close eye on the hot oil. The oil should not boil but rather heat up and have some bubbles escaping from the bottom.

Take the oil off the heat and allow it to cool for a bit. Once it is safe to touch set up a clean canning jar, funnel, and a filter of some kind. I prefer a thin square of muslin. Pour the oil through the fabric and funnel. You may want a spoon (again set aside for just this use) to drain the oil out of the left over plant material, just like you would when straining tea. You'll put your oil back into the double boiler now and prepare your beeswax. Grating the wax beforehand can be very helpful, even though the cleanup can take a while. A mixture of 1 parts wax to 5 parts oil creates a smooth mixture that easily goes onto the skin.

I add wax bit by bit why the oil is still hot in the double boiler. I test the proportions by dipping a fork in the mixture and judging the consistency by what sticks to it. Once it comes out clean with a thin layer of greasy wax I know it's ready to be put into jars.

Once the ointment has been poured into jars set them aside to cool. At this point it's important to note that throughout this process you are not just mixing herbs, oils, and wax together. You are bringing together spirits, power, and essence. When you bring together plant spirits into anything (be it potions, teas, or ointments) you should be melding the spirits that are there into something new. As an animist all things have spirit, and through the process of making flying ointment those plant spirits come together into something wholly different.

The ointment and its spirit become new allies. For some this grease can become a familiar spirit in its own right. If poured into shallow jars you should have about 3-5 jars of ointment in one session. You may want to freeze the ointments you are not using to improve their shelf life. You may also want to add other kinds of preservatives into the ointment to improve shelf life. I use clary sage oil for its associations with vision seeking but other practitioners I know have used high proof alcohol and vitamin D oil to help preserve ointments. Depending on how often you use the ointments it may be worthwhile to buy small 1-2oz tins in bulk. The smaller tins can help with preserving the oils for as long as possible, meaning you can have one tin in use while the others stay in the freezer.

Keyholes and the Skeleton Key

Contemporary witches who practice some kind of out of body experience typically use symbolism to help them navigate the otherworld. Traditional witches typically use the stang and the symbolism of a world tree as their guide and jumping off point for travel. Throughout Southern witch lore there are two interesting points within the home that possess liminal status. The chimney is used by greasy witches to fly out of the home and steal from local good stores in *The Granny Curse* while in other stories witches fly out through keyholes in order to work their witchcraft on their community. Since chimneys are less frequent than keyholes my personal practice has been much more focused on the symbol of the keyhole.

Doorways separate the wild from the domesticated. They protect us and separate us from the dangerous outside. The symbolism of the doorway can give us a gateway out of our bodies. What has been of help to me is creating a talisman out of a skeleton key to act as a key to that spiritual door. I call this talisman the skeleton key and use it in the place of the broom or stang as the tool to ride during spirit flight.

The skeleton key is cleansed and anointed with a bit of Witch's Grease. It is given its purpose and tied with cords associated with the goal of spirit flight. I make cords with a lucet and tie one to the key because it makes it easier to hold, and because it sets it aside from other keys as something special. The talisman can be worn or held during ecstatic dance or during meditation. So far the discussion of flight has exclusively included dance, but meditative practice can also lead to the slipping of the second skin.

Witches in the South often used spoken charms to help send them off. They certainly aren't alone in this, as famous Scottish witch Isobel Gowdie used the spoken phrase *"horse and hattock"* as well as the *"I shall go into a hare"* charm to shape shift and take flight. In the South there are two spoken charms that stand out for flight. One such spoken charm for flight comes from the greasy witches themselves:

"Willie Waddie, I have spoke.

Willie Waddie, remove this yoke
and let me rise like chimney smoke"

In *The Silver Bullet* there is a charm that directly talks about keyholes. *"Hi Ho Hi Ho through the keyhole I go!"* Often times folks describe what the witches say as "mumble jumble sich as we'd never heard afore"[27] so these spoken charms in English should not limit a prospective witch. You can speak in tongues or even just plain make something up if that's what works for you. Our spirits will teach us charms that can't be found in any book, charms for our lips only.

Leaving the Body without Ecstasy

Folkloric practices are not just a mirror of old stories, it is something growing and alive. While the crux of our experience comes from folklore we are surrounded by magical communities and modern magic that is entirely different. The exhausting, wild, and hair raising experiences of spirit flight are not the only way to interact with the other side. Often things like astral projection, guided meditation, and vision seeking will blend and shape how you approach out of body experiences.

Flight may not always be purposeful, hell it may not even happen while you're awake. There's plenty of contemporary and folkloric accounts of spirits dragging folks out of their bodies while they sleep. Folk witches focus on ecstatic spirit flight because of what is seen in the folklore. Flying means cackling, breaking into pubs after hours, stealing milk, dancing with the Devil, and all kinds of debauchery. While it may be controversial to say, ecstatic spirit flight is something incredibly enjoyable. That doesn't mean it's the only way to work with leaving the body. Avoid comparing your experiences to other witches.

Personal Experience with Flight and Witch's Grease

There is an unusual warmth to my body when I rub my Witch's

grease into my skin. I breathe steadily and rub the salve onto the bottom of my feet, massaging and relaxing to let the mixture do it jobs. I whisper to the ointment, call it by its name, and tell it what I want to do. *"We will come together and we will slip from this body. I will lift from my body and visit with the swamp."*

I sing Psalms to my familiars, and tell them what work we are doing. I feel their presence around me like a weighted blanket, covering me, letting me know they are ready to fly. I perform a minor ritual movement and ask for the protection of the Witch Father. I feel a tingling on my witch's mark, the place where he has claimed me, and I know I am ready.

I clothe myself making sure that each part of my body that has grease on it is well covered up. I might be a witch but even I don't have enough magical prowess to get wax and oil stains out of wall-to-wall carpeting. I wash my hands to get the grease off so nothing else gets coated. I pick up my skeleton key hanging from a cord of black, red, and white yarn. My thumb and forefinger rub up and down the cord, not unlike counting a rosary. I lay down and let my mind wander for a bit, letting all those noisy thoughts make their way up and letting them get on out.

Then I take off my skin. This always feels a bit different. Sometimes my spirit moves out of my mouth in the shape of a bird. Sometimes my spirit lifts straight out, like a classic out of body experience. Tonight I move my hands over my chest, and I feel that layer of skin trapping my spirit move out of the way. I suppose for me this is one of those mysteries, an experience that is hard to explain to someone who hasn't done it themselves. The skin is pushed aside and my spirit rises out of my body.

My spirit holds the skeleton key and walks towards a door in the room. I take a peek through the keyhole to make sure it goes where I need it to, and I see the still water of the swamp. I put the key into the hole and say "hi ho through the keyhole I go!" and I am gone. I squeeze through the hole and immediately I soar through the trees of the swamp. I can hear crickets, and gators, and birds of prey flying. I can hear laughter in the air. I follow the sounds of laughter to meet at the Sabbath, to dance for the land, to seize power from my enemies. I fly to the spirits of the swamp and the witches of this place. I fly for the joy of it, I fly for the power it brings me. I fly because I can.

Chapter Twelve

The Devil's Wife: A Note on UPG, Following Spirit, and Self Disclosure

I remember walking outside one day as a child and hearing my mom say possibly the strangest thing I've ever heard from her. "Looks like the Devil's beatin' his wife today." She was talking about the sun being our while it was raining. I never knew where this came from but I've said that phrase for almost my entire life. I've also learned that just about every other Southerner knows the same thing. The Devil has a wife, he apparently beats her, and it effects the weather. My mom has no idea why we say this, other than her mom told her and they've just always said it. We both agree it's a pretty strange thing to say. There's nothing about it in the Bible, and in the folklore no mention of exactly who this woman is.

All of these factors drove me crazy for years and I went on a hunt for the Devil's Wife. Who is she? What does she have to do with the weather? Is the Devil really beating her? What does the folklore say? These questions are in line with exactly how I experiment with my practice. This chapter explores not only my UPG, but my process for understanding folklore and the roots of the stories we tell. This kind of exploration is a wild ride and I hope it helps others embrace the guts feelings of UPG and how research helps expand on personal experience.

Who is she?

Biblically there's no mention of the Devil having a wife. There are mentions of fallen angels taking human wives, but Lucifer is never one of them. So if the Bible doesn't give me any clues, where should I turn next? Some may say Lilith from Hebrew folklore, or even Eve herself, could be likely candidates. If a Devil's Wife exists in a spiritual sense, I don't think either of those spirits foot the bill. Lilith wouldn't let someone whoop her, and Eve is firmly partnered with Adam. Eve does feature in at least one folk tale as having learned sex from the Devil, this is a creation myth about man involving Cain, but I don't think that puts her in the role of the Devil's wife[28.]

The trial of Scottish witch Agnes Naismith may give us a bit of a hint. Naismith claimed to have met with "the gentle wife of the Devil" named Antiochia. Several other witches make mention of this figure, but that's it. Just a mention of her. Or at least that's all available to me through the University of Edinburgh Witchcraft Database Survey[29]. She's always referred to as the "gentle wife" which is an interesting note.

As far as this source is concerned there are a few plausible ideas. One is that Antiochia was a local spirit known to Naismith (possibly a familiar) and during the accusations the role of "Devil's Wife" was projected onto Antiochia. This idea can be backed by some common record keeping approaches used during Scottish witch trials. Coercion via interrogators is notorious and often turns away contemporary witches from using the confessions as resources. Coercion did take place, and the records leave some key clues to determine where this takes place,[30] however, that does not mean that those being interrogated did not believe everything they confessed to. By analyzing the passages this is something that can be supported.

It could be hypothesized that Naismith knew a male spirit who imparted some knowledge to her, and that during interrogations the role of Devil was projected onto him. This was not uncommon, and can be seen in phrases by interrogators such as "the Devil, which she called X" or "he knew the Devil as X". So if Naismith then discussed this male spirit as having a wife, the interrogation may have recorded her as "the Devil's wife" in fitting with this approach. This is all conjecture as I am not a student of Scottish history nor an academic in the field of witchcraft studies, but I think that it could be plausible.

While these ideas are interesting to me as a student of anthropology it doesn't really help me in a search for who the Devil's wife is. Sure, it gives me a name, but it doesn't tell me anything about her character or much about her personality. So far this leaves me with knowing two things about her as a person, that she was called "gentle" in Scotland and that she was beaten by the Devil in America.

By looking at American folklore there is a little bit more information. One story concerning the African American folk hero Big John the Conqueror is particularly interesting. Big John flew on the back of an eagle to West Hell (which I kid you not is Florida in the story), just to take a look around. There he saw the Devil's youngest daughter and fell in love. He fought the Devil, tore off the Devil's arm, and married the Devil's youngest daughter[31.]

From this folk story we now hear that the Devil has at least two daughters (if Big Johns wife is the youngest we can assume there's at least one more) and presumably his wife gave birth to them. This can tell us that the Devil in folklore isn't just a standalone figure, he was thought to have an entire family.

Another story in the same collection gives us a little hint towards the possibility that the Devil had children with Eve in the Garden of Eden. Essentially, the story tells us that Eve learned to have sex from the Devil before she had sex with Adam. The story also implies that Cain was not Adam's son, but the Devil's and Eve's. However, Eve ends up marrying Adam and the Devil doesn't have any other interactions with her.

Folklore is a tease. It gives you just a little taste, and then never texts you back. I figured if the folklore wasn't going to give me anything else, well damn it I might as well just go find out for myself. That's been a huge point for me this entire journey, folklore is the jumping off point that I have to make something of.

What does she have to do with the Weather?

This one is short and sweet. I called up my mom to talk about this and she said "Well, I guess it's her tears [that] are the rain?" She then told me I should find some folklore about it or ask our Great Aunt. The folklore gives some regional explanations, and my mom seems to be right on the mark. The rain falling is actually the tears of the wife.

I also think it's interesting that this exact weather pattern is connected with the Devil and a Wife that no one knows anything about. Raining while the sun is shining is itself liminal. The Devil sometimes is attributed some power over storms, while the Sun is often used to describe God's light in the world. So the combining of these two at the same time adds an interesting juxtaposition for a Southern witch to look into.

This adds more meaning given some of the folk rituals that surround these showers. For instance if you put a pin in a stump during the storm you can supposedly hear the beating happening. Similarly, if you wrap a horseshoe in a white cloth and put it on the ground, then put your ear to it, you can hear the beating take place. This liminal state, with some regional rituals, allows you to listen to what takes place in Hell. As a witch I've taken this concept and run with it.

Is the Devil really beating Her?

This is a rough one on a couple levels. The elephant in the room is, this saying is awful. Domestic violence is a massive issue in the states, and unfortunately something a lot of Southerners have witnessed or been the victim of at some point. Given time I think an anthropological study could be done on the impact of folk sayings as representative of cultural norms. However I do not possess the pay grade for that particular study.

The Devil, as far as this book is concerned, is a folk-Christian term used for the Witch Father. The Witch Father can be any number of beings to any number of people but to me, the Devil in Southern folklore is a part of the Witch Father. So this phrase, and my fascination with it, creates an uncomfortable cognitive dissonance for me. Essentially, the figure of the Devil's Wife feels intimately relevant for me but the idea that the relationship between her and the Witch Father is some kind of Cosmic Domestic Violence is not one that is at all in line with the Witch Father that I have known for over ten years.

Folklore is not always literal, and I've argued that most of the highly meaningful gems we find in folklore is hidden. Folklore opens the way for us to express our Unverified Personal Gnosis (UPG). UPG basically means "this is what I've felt, and nothing says I'm wrong so I'm gonna' keep doing it. But I'm not gonna' say it's the only way to feel." UPG is our personal relationship with spirit, and really the most important part of working with spirits. The Verified Gnosis (VG) is what creates the building blocks for us to actually have our own unique practices. VG gives us common ground to come back to but our personal experience doesn't have to mirror it.

If You Ask Me,
My UPG

If you ask me, I'll tell you that the Devil has a Wife. I'll tell you that she won't be pushed around by any damn man, not even the Devil. That she isn't gettin' beat, but that both of them have such damn tempers that they go at each other like cats and dogs never givin' an inch. If you ask me, the Devil's Wife is a water woman. She takes her boat up and down Hells Rivers, she knows every dead man walking and every soul never born. Her sweat and tears are the clouds above us. She has daughters and son's I've never met and maybe never will. She don't talk much, she's too busy most of the time. She's a business woman, a boat driver, and a weather witch. She can help get you across the river, for a fair price. That's just if you ask me.

In reality, before I went searching through records to

111

"discover" the Devil's Wife, I just went to the Witch Father with some questions and he pointed me to a spirit I now associate with these sun storms. The records really didn't give me anything to go on, and I don't refer to her as Antiochia although that story stays with me. Sometimes it's better just to dive in and do something rather than wrack your brain trying to solve the riddle of it all.

To meet with or speak to the Wife, take a used horseshoe wrapped in white cloth and lay it under a pillow to use as an oracular tool. Either for prophetic dreams, or during rituals to leave the body. If it does start raining, take the rag and horseshoe and lay it on the ground. You may just hear from the Ole Lady yourself.

Take Home

This is a black sheep of a chapter because it was born out of a small phrase that I don't think is really thought about all too often. Southern folk just say it but no one really believes it from a theological stand point. I tried to be tongue in cheek for a reason, this little saying shouldn't be a big deal but it just is for me and has been the most interesting bit of UPG that I have ever encountered. Which is why I bring it up, I think that it's important to remind newly emerging witches that UPG is important! There's nothing wrong about an experience "unverified" by a source. It means something to you and as long as you acknowledge that it's from you and don't claim it's anything else - embrace it.

Chapter Thirteen

Death and Ancestors

The active inclusion of ancestors in witchcraft sets traditional and folkloric practices apart from most contemporary witchcraft practitioners. Ancestors in contemporary witchcraft typically get unpacked during Halloween and put back into a box for the rest of the year. For animists and traditional witches, ancestors are pivotal to daily practice. Ancestors are the reason why we exist and in death they can bless as easily as they can block.

Ancestor work doesn't necessarily have to be devotional or veneration, although I find most folks do venerate their dead. Sometimes ancestor work is undoing the blocks our ancestors have built. As a witch it is quite possible that your ancestors will have some issues with what you are doing. It is also possible your ancestors are just happy to hear from you.

Beginning an ancestral practice is simple and personal. No one can tell you how to venerate your ancestors, but there are some starting points that help most folks get started. Pictures, candles, and personal belongings of an ancestors placed on a table is how most folks start. Simply talking to the ancestors brings them closer. Communicating with ancestors can be done in many ways, typically starting with a familiar form of divination can open the way. Different regions, cultures, and religions will have their own traditions surrounding ancestral veneration. Due to the deeply personal nature of this practice I encourage each witch to search on their own, create their own practice, rather than copy one out of a book.

Sunday evenings I take the time to go to my magic room and shut out the world around me. I put on my favorite Dolly Parton album, *Little Sparrow*, and start lighting candles. I tell my Papi how his daughter is doing, tell my cousins what's new, and spend the evening talking to my other beloved dead. I sing along while I crochet, or weave cords, or wood burn spirit boards. I listen to the words that my dead have for me. Most are curious, but flighty.

My ancestors are respectful of my work but just like my living family very few are involved with my work. They may know that I curse and I bless, but they don't spectate or get involved. Some, long dead before I or my parents ever knew them, come forward and offer advice. Some, farther back even, come forward as strong allies.

For the ancestors who are there to spend time with their grandchild, I offer words and cornbread, maybe a dash of whiskey. For my ancestors who add to my witchcraft I offer necklaces of precious beads and tools made from deer hooves to help work our wills together. Every household and every person is different.

Within my household my partner has his own ancestral practice. He keeps fresh water and a white candle near photos of his Puerto Rican aguela and his Florida Cracker grandpa. He talks to them and refills the water. He sprinkles Florida Water on the altar and himself. His altar is prominently displayed in our living room, while mine is privately held in a separate room. No two ancestral practices will ever look the same or mean the same things. No one can tell you how an ancestral practice can be conducted except your ancestors.

The Ancestors' Skull

Sitting on my altar is a skull filled to the brim with plants and stones meant to support my ancestors, to give them a place to work their magic. Only my ancestors who have made it clear that they want to be involved in my witchcraft have access to this skull. The skull is made into a centerpiece when I am seeking visions about a certain event. I will light candles, mutter charms, and open the skull to these ancestors. I will light and inhale fumes from an incense blend designed to help see visions. I will ask my ancestors to guide these visions and show me what I am looking for.

This skull also features as a supportive tool in other works. When I fly I often ask my ancestors and certain familiars to watch over my body, and the skull gives them an anchor to do so. Without an anchor the ancestors can still bring us blessings and signs, but these anchors give them the ability to do so directly and more frequently.

The Underworld

The relationship between witches and death is an intimate one. In folklore, witches are often harbingers of death, taking lives by whipping up storms at sea or sluggin' witchballs at those who violate hospitality. Contemporary witches often address death on friendly terms, understanding it as an unavoidable facet of life. Folkloric witches sit at a crux to both claim the powers of death and keep them at bay.

Witchcraft allows us to change the physical world through spells, talismans, and our familiars. Witchcraft also allows us to change the spiritual world through will, frenzy, and spirit flight. When a witch begins an ancestral practice the boundaries between the living and the dead start to fade. It may become clear that our bodies are themselves spirit houses, and we are the spirits inhabiting them. Our ancestors then are not just spirits we contact because they are related to us, but also because they can guide us into the realm of the dead.

Flying to the underworld is a practice that most folks talk about as inherently dangerous and not to be tread on lightly. These are fair warnings, as the underworld seems to be perpetually hungry for new guests. However as witches who embrace their own autonomy, power, and wildness a sense of danger is to be expected. When our spirit flight practice has matured and our relationship with the dead has become well defined, there is a strong possibility that the underworld is going to become a travel destination.

Whereas a witch may fly to the Sabbath for the pure joy of it, underworld flying tends to be a bit more calculated. The underworld doesn't like to let go, and so you may run the risk of leaving something behind each time. This is a reminder that witchcraft is a dangerous path as much as it is an empowering one. The largest benefit to flying to the underworld is knowledge of how to improve life in the physical world. The land of the dead can teach you how to heal directly, but also how to send sickness spirits to the underworld to be eaten.

Going to the underworld is no more difficult than flying anywhere else, once the talent has been developed. The difference here is, to beat a dead horse, the risk involved. There are bits of folklore that can help this though, as well as some of my own UPG that has helped me in the past. One saying that stands out in the South is: you'll never see a blue jay on Fridays because that's the day they go to Hell to tell the Devil what they've seen. A different blue jay related piece of folklore I heard growing up is that if you see a blue jay it means a dead loved one is protecting you in heaven. Both of these sayings relate blue jays to death and one even gives us a day on which we may fly with the jays to visit the dead ourselves.

Southern folklore also gives us a heaping of ways to protect ourselves from ghosts that can be twisted a bit to protect ourselves while in the land of ghosts. The haint tree is a well-known Southern tool for protecting a house against ghosts, and I figure if it's good enough for the whole family it's good enough for me too. So I threw together a haint charm made with a small antique blue bottle tied to a cord and hung around my neck during spirit flight with the simple direction of "make sure my spirit comes back to this body in one piece."

If you go to any antique store they're liable to have old bitters bottles lying around. These are brightly colored glass bottles about two to three inches tall and feature all kinds of interesting images. Most will run you about three dollars, but I've haggled them down to as low as fifty cents a bottle before. You'll consecrate them to their purpose in the same ritual format as the spirit house but with a different purpose. Leave the bottle empty and uncorked, so you can rush back into it if things turn sour. Alternatively, fill it with soil from your lawn so you always return home.

The final piece of the puzzle is the presence of our ancestors. Our ancestors know the realm of the dead as well as we know our towns here on earth. They can vouch for us among other spirits, keep us on the right paths, and make sure we make it home intact. When traveling to the underworld our ancestors become our protectors and our shepherds. Eventually we may learn the underworlds topography for ourselves and venture on our own, but like any strange new place it's always nice to have a familiar face to help us along.

To Fly with Blue Jays

We start on a Friday when we know the jays will be flying underground to give secrets to the Devil and the dead. Tie your protective charm, like a haint charm, around your neck and remind it of its purpose. Call your dead and your familiars to your side, telling them what you are doing. Rub your Witch's Grease on yourself and sing songs of the underworld. Ask your familiars to protect your body, and your ancestors to guide your spirit.

Start your trance process and look for a flock of jays. When you close your eyes and send your spirit out, listen for their songs. Be aware of any dead relatives who have taken the form of a blue jay, ask them to lend you their shape to fly to the underworld. When your spirit leaves your skin take the form of the blue jay and join their flock. Sing while you fly with them, but be mindful not to offend them or get on their bad sides. Blue jays are notoriously nasty when provoked. Be prepared to pay the toll that all the other jays pay, a secret from the land of the living. The jays aren't just there to sight see, they come offerings secrets to the dead. Something as simple as office gossip is enough to tantalize them and help pay your way underground.

Fly with them down into the underworld, where you will notice that things seem just a little off. Plants grow in ways that shouldn't be possible, animals may walk backwards, and humans may have no faces. Many people experience the underworld differently, but I have always noticed it is just a bit backwards for us living folks.

Land and take back your form, calling to your ancestors to walk with you. Remind your ancestors of the specific reason why you flew down into the underworld. If it's to bring back knowledge of healing they may bring you to a specific dead who can instruct you in healing. If it is to cast out sickness spirits they may bring you to a particularly nasty pit that you can throw a spirit into. You may ask them to teach you how to eat spirits, how to enter someone's dreams, or how to conjure the dead into your world. There is no guarantee that the dead will show you these things for free, so be sure to negotiate a payment before you are shown anything. Think back to old fairy tales, loose ends always end up bad for the heroes. Be specific, be clear, be direct.

Only ask for one thing at a time (no need to rack up debt) and return home. Fly back the way you came and record everything that took place. The underworld has an interesting effect on the memory in my experience and it's best to get it all out while it's still fresh. Make your payments as soon as possible, be true to your word because I can assure that they will remember what you agreed to and take it by whatever means possible.

Riding the Ferry of the Devil's Wife

I spoke earlier about how in my UPG the Devil Wife is a kind of psychopomp, a spirit who knows the dead and guides them to the underworld. Think Charon from Greek mythology but less dour. From my interactions with this spirit, the Devil's Wife has made a business out of her position in the underworld and will gladly give anyone safe passage to the underworld for a bit of coin. All of the following should be driven home: these are my personal experiences, I don't claim them to be historically/ folklorically accurate, but it has damn sure worked for me.

There is a system to talking to the Devil's Wife. Slather on some Witch's Grease, get you a horseshoe and two quarters. Put the horseshoe on a white cloth, place the two quarters in between the horns of the shoe and wrap it all up in the rag. Place the cloth under your pillow and fly to the Devil's Wife. Tell her where you need to go, what you need to learn, and what you have to pay her (the two quarters). She'll either accept the offer or tell you that the price isn't right and ask for more. Negotiate well and she'll take you to your destination, and possibly offer some tips along the way.

When you arrive at your destination repeat your call to the ancestors as described above and finish out whatever business you came there to do. A separate payment will be needed for the knowledge attained. When you're done the Devil's Wife will take you safely back to where you came from.

I'm very cautious about how I put out my UPG because it has been so common over the years for witchy folks to present their personal experiences as historical fact and that is something I will always strive to avoid. I do however think it's important to show in one small way how my UPG has worked and how the folklore has given me a starting place, but I don't allow folklore to block my progress in my craft. Another pitfall of presenting UPG is that spirits are notoriously secretive, and if you are given knowledge it is very likely they will demand secrecy from you at the cost of taking their knowledge back from you. When I asked the Devil's Wife during my trance work how she would feel about me discussing her in a book I received this message: "You mean to tell me that you're putting public information out there about me, and there may even be people who read about me and want to give me more money? If I don't get put in that book I ain't never takin' your sorry ass across the water ever again."

Chapter Fourteen

The Witch Father of Southern Cunning

The Witch Father is not an easy figure to talk about. The Witch Father is not even a singular entity at all. There are many, probably countless, spirits that make witches. I find it unlikely that who I call the Witch Father matches up to the one the reader may call to. The Devil, Satan, Lucifer, Pan, Azazel, Cernunnos, and Old Scratch are all Witch Fathers. Some folk think they're all the same, I don't reckon they are. When I talk about the Witch Father for myself, I'm talking about The Black Woodsman. *The Silver Bullet* describes The Black Woodsman as a tall black man with long curly hair wielding an axe[32]. In the story he shows a greedy old man where to find treasure at the price of the man's soul. While it is a good story, and the name fits the Witch Father, this is not the relationship I have with him.

The Black Woodsman is the devil of the trees. He is the bridge between what is wild and dangerous reaching out towards humans. He is not feral, but he is not tame. He wields lightning and claims what is his. From the weak he claims souls, from the strong he claims loyalty. In witches, he can stoke the fire and ride with them on the Wild Hunt. In the same story he reveals another of his names, the Wild Huntsman.

The Black Woodsman is my devil, my Witch Father, the one who found me as a child and took me on my first Hunt. He is who guides me on this journey. Who has taken from me, eaten me, and built me. I have eaten from him and fought with him. He has humored me and drank with me. He is not the same as Satan though many have called him that. He is not Cernunnos though even I have called him that. He is an American devil and makes American witches.

He is not an infallible god. He has been tricked by the ones who he has given his cunning fire to. He is as funny as he is demanding. He can be lighthearted and stern. I do not view the Black Woodsman as a terrifying figure to bow down to. I respect him as a father, one who is experienced and worthy of respect and loyalty. That does not mean we always agree. He has a secret name he has told me and etched onto my heart. For now we will do well to say that the Witch Father of Southern Cunning is The Black Woodsman.

Your Witch Father may have horns or scales or wings. He may be She of the stars, or the dirt, or the sea. They may come to you in many shapes and sizes and varying levels of humanity. They may be spirits of the land, or of blood, or of spirit. I cannot tell you who your Witch Initiator will be. I cannot tell you who you familiar will be. I cannot tell you what your initiation may be like. Do not try and make your experience mimic any other witches, least of all mine. Read this book and dozens more like it. Learn from them and learn from others. Use what resonates, but don't try to mimic.

Read the folklore, use what resonates, but don't try to mimic. If what you hear in folklore does not feel organic in your hands, it is not right for you. When the spirits come to you, when The Witch Father lights a fire in you, when you know what you need to do without turning to a book- that is when you are a witch.

Closing Thoughts

Being a witch is something that will never fully make sense. We are never going to agree on what it means to be a witch or what the experience of a witch is. I think that gets to the heart of being a witch. We are diverse creatures, filled with a fire and made something different by our relationship with the other side. We speak to the dead, we have died and been put back together. We change and bend the reality around us in subtle and meaningful ways.

For a while now we have been told there is only one way to be a witch. We have been told to seek teachers and initiations in order to be truly a witch. Our thoughts have been stripped from us. We have been told to accept a false history with no questions, no research on our behalf. We have relegated the spirits of witchcraft to associations and correspondences, we have attempted to strip them of their autonomy and ourselves of our claws.

This path is about getting back our claws and rediscovering the faces of the spirits. I have left others for a lonely path so that I can ask my own questions and do my own research. My findings, my mistakes, my connections belong to me. I take ownership of every misstep. I don't offer it to anything else, I take accountability for what I've done.

Southern witchcraft is not the only part of my practice, but it is by far the most underrepresented part of my practice. That is a huge part of why this book has been made. To inspire other Southerners that there is validity in our home towns. Our backyards are just as full of magic as the fields of the British countryside. The South is diverse. The South is black, the South is Latino, the South is white, the South is indigenous. It should not be assumed that the witches in these stories are all white, nor should these stories be used to press any kind of Southern pride that equates whiteness. Southernness is about hospitality, a mixed heritage, and an acceptance of a dark past.

My hope is that witches continue on a path that is inspired. Witches are moving in many directions, all of them are seeking something powerful. If someone reads this book and finds that power, that's wonderful. My real goal though is that someone reads this book and finds power in their own story.

Tool Index

Here I outline the tools used in this practice both magical and practical. The methods of creation are peppered throughout the book but I thought this short list would be useful for reference as well as a potential shopping list. Most everything in the book can be found around the house or in your area, but some folks might need to look to shops to buy tools so having everything on one page should make that trip a little easier.

Magical

Bible: Much of Southern folk magic revolves around the use of the bible. Most of what I write about concerning the bible I witnessed throughout my childhood. While I call it magic, my family would call it superstitions or looking for help from God. The bible can either be used to incorporate a Christian upbringing or to desecrate a Christian upbringing. Many traditional witchcraft initiations include revoking God and claiming the power of the bible for the Devil. I find this completely valid, but not something I use. I find that my Christian upbringing had some magic in it, and although I left the church and belief in the Christian God, I still think magic courses in the Bible. This is a long line of traditions seen in folk magic and ceremonial magic alike. The charms of Psalms in particular can be used in amazing ways.

Black Book: I distinguish this and the Bible so there isn't confusion, but the historical fact is there very little distinguishing or clarification in the folklore. Sometimes the Black Book is the Devil's book containing signatures of other witches, sometimes it is a grimoire of magic, and sometimes it is a bible with a red X in the book of revelations. For me, I use it as a grimoire. A container of only my most useful information and successful workings. I have plenty of notebooks filled with thoughts, ramblings, and experimentations but only one Black Book. The Black Book is what I consider direct connection to my gnosis and possibly what I would consider passing on in my family because I know what's in that book will always work.

Broom: In this practice the creation of the broom is a link to the spirits of the land. Among traditional witches, brooms mostly feature as tools for spirit flight. Southern folklore gives that job to grease and hats. For folkloric witches brooms are made of local material, and should be made by hand. The broom here acts as a way to speak with land spirits more directly and illicit help in cleansing and protection.

Cards/Divination Tool: it is recommended that a witch have some kind of divination practice. This acts as our life line to the spirit world. Although a lot of what you're doing will open you up to spirit communication and mediumship, it isn't guaranteed. Divination can give us an objective way to speak with spirits. Playing cards are talked about in folklore and folk practices, but almost anything can be used. Recently I've experimented with personal divination and bone tossing. Like most things in this book, look to the lore but don't get stuck in the mud.

Conjure Bone: the single most important talisman in this practice. The creation of which is detailed earlier, this talisman become our "good luck charm" and generator of power. Everyone's will be different, and even the functions differ. My time working with this tool has revealed that it is one part symbol of authority, one part battery of power, and one part familiar spirit. It is the crossroads of this approach and is integral to mixing with spirits and getting tuned into our magical practice.

Devil's Club: this is an offensive tool made by bundling together thorny sticks. The Devil's club is often used to strike an effigy of an enemy who is trying to harm you or your family through magic. Contemporary witchcraft traditions often use a knife, wand, or blasting rod as a means to clear an area of negative influence and the Devil's Club can be utilized in similar ways. On the occasion that a nasty spirit is interfering with you this is the tool to turn to. It should be noted that unlike other contemporary magical traditions, this magical weapon only fulfills a defensive/offensive role and it should be clear to your working partners (either spirits or other witches) why you are using it at a given time.

Focus: This is usually a small to medium sized wooden disk used to focus on a particular object. Depending on the design, this can also function as a semi-permanent Thin Place to be used in spirit flight or calling the Witch Father. To signal my intention to start working I knock three times on the disk and start saying hello to my spirits.

Horseshoe: horseshoes are almost synonymous with Southern homes. Often hung above doorways to bring good luck, the Horseshoe stands as a powerful protective talisman. Some stories tell that a witch (for us an enemy or any baring ill will) cannot enter a home forwards if a horseshoe is hung over the door. It attracts luck and keeps the home safe, and should always be hung "horns up". Should the shoe fall or swing down, either cleans or dispose of it. I keep a horseshoe on my altar and use it as a cleansing tool in situations where burning herbs may not be appropriate. Keep in mind, some spirits are offended or harmed by iron. Depending on the spirits around you a horseshoe may not be appropriate. Particularly if you work with the Good Neighbors, commonly called fairies. While not all Good Neighbors seem to be bothered by iron, in almost all folklore they are shown to have a major aversion to the substance. When in doubt, consult your divination tools.

A little known bit of folklore is that when it's still sunny during a thunderstorm you can take a horseshoe wrapped in white cloth, lay it on the ground, put your ear to it and hear the Devil beating his wife. This sounds horrific and I tackle this little legend in its own chapter. The tool though, the shoe wrapped in cloth, can be used as an oracular device to trigger visionary dreams.

Skeleton Key: a simple talisman used as a focus for spirit flight work. This tool replaces the stang or broom of other traditions as the main vehicle for spirit flight. This tool is most effective when using the imagery of a universal door and keyhole to slip through. I dress mine with a black, red, and white cord made of yarn. Although I prefer skeleton keys for aesthetic and symbolic purposes, any key (including your car keys) could be used.

Silver Bullet: while this can be a literal silver bullet, I use the term to mean any piece of silver used during the Killing the Moon ritual. This may be a tool that is only used once and is then disposed of after the ritual. For me, I can't normally just throw out silver- even if it's for witchcraft. I also find that this tool is deeply infused with power after the ritual and use it in my daily practice. I don't think that the Silver Bullet has to be one certain thing. I find that being so deeply infused with the ritual gives the Silver Bullet a lot of variability just like the Conjure Bone. I think the one role it can fulfill most strongly is protective, especially if it is a literal bullet.

Witch's Grease: an herbal concoction slathered onto the body that makes moving in the second skin possible. The herbs used are dictated by spirit, most have entheogenic origins. All herbs should be heavily researched before use.

Witchballs: There are two kinds of witchballs, in this book I talk about the wax balls not the glass ones. Witchball's are used to curse, plain and simple.

Animal Parts: literally all parts of an animal can be used in magic. Skulls can be turned into spirit homes, bones can be included in divination, and furs can be used for shape shifting or to throw divination tools onto. The qualities of the animal will determine how they are used and are unique to each one.

Rabbits Foot: a classic good luck charm that can be used by keeping it on a person's body. There are certain rituals that involve catching the rabbit in a graveyard before the foot can be taken. Another option is to take a foot that has already been removed (humanely) and taking it to a graveyard to imbue it with luck.

Chicken Feet: These can be used for a variety of purposes. In my craft I use them as bases for wands, which I rarely use in my practice. They can also be bases for other talismans, particularly in glamours. Tied with a red thread and worn under your shirt, chicken feet can be used to evoke lust from others.

Porcupine Quills: can be used in binding spells to stop movement of an enemy. Can be implemented into a Devil's Club. They can also be inscribed with psalms or spells to protect a home.

Practical

Alcohol: Herbal tinctures can be infused in high-proof alcohol. And most spirits enjoy a good nip of whiskey now and again. I try to always keep a little whiskey and grain alcohol lying around.

Asafetida: a sulfur smelling plant extract used in reversing curses and banishing witches.

Cast Iron Pot/Fire Proof Container: Use this to burn your herbs in. I prefer cast iron because as a Southern I know that Cast Iron is very versatile. The tradition that you don't wash a cast iron skillet translates very well into magic. Some families have skillets at least a hundred years old, never washed once. Every young Southerner knows you have to season your first skillet because it doesn't have the goodness of your granny's old one. These skillets remember every dish ever made and brings that to the table, soap would get rid of all those years of goodness. I think the same applies to a good cast iron burning pot. The pot remembers the spells you've cast into it and tinctures you brewed in it. You might scrub it with salt or a rough pad to get gunk off between dishes/spells, but let all that magical goodness soak over the years.

Mortar and Pestle/food processor: Herbs play a major role in practical magic and the mortar and pestle is my most used tool in my practice. While I do consider it to be practical, over the years I have begun to see it as something profoundly magical. As an animist I view all things as having spirit, and so when I blend different plants and herbs into a mortar, something very interesting happens. A new spirit comes forward to assist me in my work. These new spirits are very different from the source spirits, like a child would be different from its parents. This is why I personally do not use a food processor to replace my mortar and pestle. While it is more efficient, I personally do not feel as though my personal power mingles with the plant spirits the way it does when I'm physically grinding them. Besides, a little elbow grease never hurt no one.

Mason Jars: What can these be used for? Everything. Buy a whole flat of these little buggers. Witch jars, herb closets, spirit homes, pickling - they can be used for anything.

Paper: Paper can be used for damn near anything in magic. Write a psalm on a piece of paper and stick it in your pocket to attract money. Write a verse down and throw it in your shoe to make sure your heading in the right direction. There is a particular practice of "writing tickets" in the Appalachian Mountains that concerns writing a particular phrase on paper, drilling a hold in a particular tree, stuffing an iron rod into the tree, and smacking the Jesus out of that rod with a hammer. This is done to heal, get rid of hexes, and a few other things.[37]

There are also written charms that have nothing to do with the Bible, namely Abracadabra and the Sator Square. In *The Silver Bullet* Abracadabra is used for clairvoyance to find a lost object. Normally I've seen it used as a protective charm written in defending order. Sator Squares are old as sin and have been found in both Pompeii and Appalachia[38]. I use clay for Sator Squares and hide them around the house as a protective talisman, and sometimes as a spirit trap.

Wood Burner: I never considered myself an artistic person because I can't draw for a lick. But the first time I decided I would use a wood burner for a spirit board, I realized art isn't just drawing and painting. Wood burning magical tools is therapeutic, creative, magical, and beautiful. Of course it isn't a necessity but I encourage all witches to explore artistic endeavors that can also express their craft.

Sulfur: used in all kinds of protective magic but particularly getting rid of nasty spirits or witches.

Footnotes

1. Davis, Hubert J. (1975) *The Silver Bullet and other American Witch Stories,* 16
2. Davis, Hubert J. (1975) *The Silver Bullet and other American Witch Stories,* 61
3. Milnes, Gerald C. (2007) *Signs, Cures, & Witchery,* 178
4. Lawless, http://sarahannelawless.com/2015/05/17/catching-and-binding-spirits/
5. Davis, Hubert J. (1975) *The Silver Bullet and other American Witch Stories,* 34
6. Davis, Hubert J. (1975) *The Silver Bullet and other American Witch Stories,* 91
7. Hatsis, Thomas (2015) *The Witches' Ointment the Secret History of Psychedelic Magic,* 124
8. Davis, Hubert J. (1975) *The Silver Bullet and other American Witch Stories,* 31
9. Davis, Hubert J. (1975) *The Silver Bullet and other American Witch Stories,* 141
10. Davies, Owen (2009) *Grimoires A History of Magic Books,* 82
11. Davis, Hubert J. (1975) *The Silver Bullet and other American Witch Stories,* 191
12. Hutcherson, Cory Thomas (2014) Essay *Killing the Moon Witchcraft Initiations in the Mountains of The Southern United States* in the anthology *Hands of Apostasy* edited by Michael Howard and Daniel A. Schulke, 38
13. Hutcherson, Cory Thomas (2014) Essay *Killing the Moon Witchcraft Initiations in the Mountains of The Southern United States* in the anthology *Hands of Apostasy* edited by Michael Howard and Daniel A. Schulke, 64
14. I should note that animal abuse and animal sacrifice are not the same. What is described in these stories is abuse plain and simple. Animal sacrifice is done with great respect to the

animals and very rarely is it done with animals that are not already avidly consumed by most people (pigs, chickens, goats, bulls). Animals sacrifice, when done by people who have been trained in the practice or were raised in cultures that utilize it, is a humbling experience and is a steadfast reminder that we would not exist without our livestock. None of those things are even hinted at in the story of the black cat.

15. Milnes, Gerald C. (2007) *Signs, Cures, & Witchery*, 149
16. Not looking behind you after completing a working is a pretty old bit of advice, one that I attribute to either to the story of Sodom or Orpheus. I say rearview mirrors are the exception because of basic safety concerns. And there is a bit of lore surrounding mirrors and navigating around magical taboos.
17. Wilby, Emma (2005) *Cunning Folk and Familiar Spirits*, 68
18. The Survey of Scottish Witchcraft, The University of Edinburgh, http://www.shca.ed.ac.uk/Research/witches/
19. Wilby, Emma (2005) *Cunning Folk and Familiar Spirits*, 68
20. http://www.infinite-beyond.com/down-at-the-crossroads/
21. Davis, Hubert J. (1975) *The Silver Bullet and other American Witch Stories*, 16
22. Hatsis, Thomas (2015) *The Witches' Ointment the Secret History of Psychedelic Magic*, 77
23. Wilby, Emma (2005) *Cunning Folk and Familiar Spirits*, 61
24. Wilby, Emma (2005) *Cunning Folk and Familiar Spirits*, 245
25. Lawless, http://sarahannelawless.com/resources/introduction-to-flying-ointments/
26. Davis, Hubert J. (1975) *The Silver Bullet and other American Witch Stories*, 18
27. Davis, Hubert J. (1975) *The Silver Bullet and other American Witch Stories*, 16
28. Kennedy, Stetson (1942) *Palmetto Country*, 158
29. The Survey of Scottish Witchcraft, The University of

Edinburgh, http://www.shca.ed.ac.uk/Research/witches/

30. Wilby (2010) *The Visions of Isobel Gowdie Magic, Witchcraft and Dark Shamanism in Seventeenth-Century Scotland*, 53

31. Kennedy, Stetson (1942) *Palmetto Country*, 153

32. Davis, Hubert J. (1975) *The Silver Bullet and other American Witch Stories*, 151

Sources

Davis, Hubert J. (1975) *The Silver Bullet and other American Witch Stories*

Hatsis, Thomas (2015) *The Witches' Ointment the Secret History of Psychedelic Magic*

Arrow, Jan (1987) *By Southern Hands a Celebration of Craft Traditions in the South*

Morgan, Lee (2013) *A Deed Without a Name: Unearthing a Legacy of Traditional Witchcraft*

Wilby, Emma (2005) *Cunning Folk and Familiar Spirits*

Milnes, Gerald C. (2007) *Signs, Cures, & Witchery*

Russell, Randy:Barnet, Janet (1999) *The Granny Curse and Other Ghost Stories and Legends from East Tennessee*

Hutcherson, Cory Thomas: Laine of *New World Witchery* Podcast

Hutcherson, Cory Thomas (2013) *Fifty-Four Devils*

Hutcherson, Cory Thomas (2014) Essay *Killing the Moon Witchcraft Initiations in the Mountains of The Southern United States* in the anthology *Hands of Apostasy* edited by Michael Howard and Daniel A. Schulke

Kennedy, Stetson (1942) *Palmetto Country*

Randolph, Vance (1947) *Ozark Magic and Folklore*

Davies, Owen (2009) *Grimoires A History of Magic Books*

Chris Orapello of *Down at the Crossroads* Podcast

Recommended Books for Southern Witches

The Silver Bullet Compiled by Hurbert J. Davis

Ozark Magic and Folklore by Vance Randolph

The Granny Curse by Randy Russell and Janet Barnet

Signs, Cures, and Witchery by Gerald C. Milnes

By Southern Hands a Celebration of Craft Traditions in the South by Jan Arrow

Killing the Moon; Witchcraft Initiations in the Mountains of The

Southern United States by Cory Hutcherson in the anthology *Hands of Apostasy* edited by Michael Howard and Daniel A. Schulke

Palmetto Country by Stetson Kennedy)

Southern Jack Tales by Donald Davis

The Holy Bible

Books for folkloric witches

A Deed Without a Name: Unearthing a Legacy of Traditional Witchcraft by Lee Morgan

Cunning Folk and Familiar Spirits by Emma Wilby

The Visions of Isobel Gowdie by Emma Wilby

Any book relating to your local lore, plants, and animals

MOON
BOOKS

PAGANISM & SHAMANISM

What is Paganism? A religion, a spirituality, an alternative belief system, nature worship? You can find support for all these definitions (and many more) in dictionaries, encyclopaedias, and text books of religion, but subscribe to any one and the truth will evade you. Above all Paganism is a creative pursuit, an encounter with reality, an exploration of meaning and an expression of the soul. Druids, Heathens, Wiccans and others, all contribute their insights and literary riches to the Pagan tradition. Moon Books invites you to begin or to deepen your own encounter, right here, right now.

If you have enjoyed this book, why not tell other readers by posting a review on your preferred book site.

Recent bestsellers from Moon Books are:

Journey to the Dark Goddess
How to Return to Your Soul
Jane Meredith
Discover the powerful secrets of the Dark Goddess and transform your depression, grief and pain into healing and integration.
Paperback: 978-1-84694-677-6 ebook: 978-1-78099-223-5

Shamanic Reiki
Expanded Ways of Working with Universal Life Force Energy
Llyn Roberts, Robert Levy
Shamanism and Reiki are each powerful ways of healing; together, their power multiplies. Shamanic Reiki introduces techniques to

help healers and Reiki practitioners tap ancient healing wisdom.
Paperback: 978-1-84694-037-8 ebook: 978-1-84694-650-9

Pagan Portals – The Awen Alone

Walking the Path of the Solitary Druid
Joanna van der Hoeven
An introductory guide for the solitary Druid, The Awen Alone
will accompany you as you explore, and seek out your own place
within the natural world.
Paperback: 978-1-78279-547-6 ebook: 978-1-78279-546-9

A Kitchen Witch's World of Magical Herbs & Plants

Rachel Patterson
A journey into the magical world of herbs and plants, filled with
magical uses, folklore, history and practical magic. By popular
writer, blogger and kitchen witch, Tansy Firedragon.
Paperback: 978-1-78279-621-3 ebook: 978-1-78279-620-6

Medicine for the Soul

The Complete Book of Shamanic Healing
Ross Heaven
All you will ever need to know about shamanic healing and how to
become your own shaman...
Paperback: 978-1-78099-419-2 ebook: 978-1-78099-420-8

Traditional Witchcraft for the Woods and Forests

A Witch's Guide to the Woodland with Guided Meditations and
Pathworking
Melusine Draco
A Witch's guide to walking alone in the woods, with guided
meditations and pathworking.
Paperback: 978-1-84694-803-9 ebook: 978-1-84694-804-6

Wild Earth, Wild Soul
A Manual for an Ecstatic Culture
Bill Pfeiffer
Imagine a nature-based culture so alive and so connected,
spreading like wildfire. This book is the first flame…
Paperback: 978-1-78099-187-0 ebook: 978-1-78099-188-7

Naming the Goddess
Trevor Greenfield
Naming the Goddess is written by over eighty adherents and
scholars of Goddess and Goddess Spirituality.
Paperback: 978-1-78279-476-9 ebook: 978-1-78279-475-2

Readers of ebooks can buy or view any of these bestsellers by
clicking on the live link in the title. Most titles are published in
paperback and as an ebook. Paperbacks are available in traditional
bookshops. Both print and ebook formats are available online.

Find more titles and sign up to our readers' newsletter at
http://www.johnhuntpublishing.com/paganism
Follow us on Facebook at https://www.facebook.com/MoonBooks
and Twitter at https://twitter.com/MoonBooksJHP

What people are saying about

Southern Cunning

Get your cast iron pots and asafetida ready, it's time to fly! Aaron Oberon is inviting you on an eye-opening trip to his home - where, as he says, backyards are just as full of magic as the fields of the British countryside. This book presents a practical view of witchcraft in the oft-ignored and wildly misunderstood American South, full of regional folklore and Oberon's individual experience - not to mention some truly fun spellwork.
Tara-Love Maguire, co-author of *Besom, Stang, and Sword* and co-host of the Down at the Crossroads podcast

Aaron Oberon has written a virtual means and methods primer for the modern folkloric witch as they make their way along the shifting landscape of witchcraft in today's world.
Christopher Orapello, co-author of *Besom, Stang, and Sword* and co-host of the Down at the Crossroads podcast

Southern Cunning is a much needed and fascinating look at the practice of American folkloric witchcraft. Practical and imaginative, wise and engaging, Oberon's book is essential reading for anyone interested in traditional witchcraft or southern folklore.
Morgan Daimler, author of *The Morrigan, Fairies* and *Fairy Witchcraft*

A straight-talking, easy to follow take on folkloric witchcraft from the South, rich in personal anecdotes and practical tips.
Lee Morgan, author of *A Deed Without a Name* and *Standing and Not Falling*

This is the sort of book I wish there were more of, because it connects the living magic of the past with the living magic of the present without getting stuck on problems of lineage, authentication, or secrecy. *Southern Cunning* will be a valuable addition to the library of anyone with an interest in folklore, magic, and witches with a Southern flavor.

Cory Thomas Hutcheson, host of the podcast New World Witchery